M000023235

How Video Games Impact Players

How Video Games Impact Players

The Pitfalls and Benefits of a Gaming Society

Ryan Rogers

LEXINGTON BOOKS
Lanham • Boulder • New York • London

Published by Lexington Books
An imprint of The Rowman & Littlefield Publishing Group, Inc.
4501 Forbes Boulevard, Suite 200, Lanham, Maryland 20706
www.rowman.com

Unit A, Whitacre Mews, 26-34 Stannary Street, London SE11 4AB

Copyright © 2016 by Lexington Books

All rights reserved. No part of this book may be reproduced in any form or by any electronic or mechanical means, including information storage and retrieval systems, without written permission from the publisher, except by a reviewer who may quote passages in a review.

British Library Cataloguing in Publication Information Available

Library of Congress Cataloging-in-Publication Data

Library of Congress Cataloging-in-Publication Data

Names: Rogers, Ryan
Title: How video games impact players : the pitfalls and benefits of a gaming society / Ryan Rogers.
Description: Lanham : Lexington Books, [2016]
Identifiers: LCCN 2016011886| ISBN 9781498513074 (cloth : alk. paper) | ISBN 9781498513081 (electronic)
Subjects: LCSH: Video games—Social aspects.
Classification: LCC GV1469.17.S63 R64 2016 | DDC 794.8—dc23 LC record available at https://lccn.loc.gov/2016011886

♾ ™ The paper used in this publication meets the minimum requirements of American National Standard for Information Sciences Permanence of Paper for Printed Library Materials, ANSI/NISO Z39.48-1992.

Printed in the United States of America

Dedicated to Mom and Dad, for all the support you gave, lessons you shared, and games we played.

Contents

Introduction

*Why Games Are Important, and Who Is Playing
Video Games?*

The purpose of this book is to provide an overview of how video games impact their players. More specifically, this book aims to provide a discussion of these effects within the context of essential game elements—that is, how the game is designed. While there is no shortage of books on video games and books on critical elements of game design, the two are rarely combined since the two domains are typically treated as separate entities.

This book takes the position that one is important to the other. A deeper understanding of social issues in games requires knowing how the game is designed. Simultaneously understanding how a game is designed requires knowing the effects. For example, a study on problematic portrayals of gender in video games is enlightening, and there are many studies on the topic that will be discussed in the following pages that have helped to advance our knowledge, however it is important to consider: how are those gender portrayals programmed into the game? Certainly we would expect the social repercussions to be different if the player is controlling a sexualized character versus the sexualized character being a part of the background. Likewise, what if the player is competing with a sexualized character as opposed to cooperating with a sexualized character? More often than not, the design elements and the social issues in video games have a bearing on one another. This book aims to combine those two worlds for a meaningful, and hopefully informative, analysis of the effects of video games. Before getting into that analysis, a bit of background on the video game industry is necessary.

It is tempting to dismiss video games as "kids' stuff" or a "waste of time." However, video games play a vital role in contemporary society. According to the Entertainment Software Association, an organization dedicated to serving and promoting the video game industry (this includes games on the Internet, game consoles, and personal computers), more than half of United States citizens plays video games (Entertainment Software Association, 2014). Even though game sales are down from recent years (Takahashi, 2014), likely due to economic recession and the release of new console hardware, the video game industry sold more than 20 billion dollars worth of hardware and software in 2013 (Entertainment Software Association, 2014). From purely a financial perspective, video games are an important factor in American, Japanese, and European economies. Daniel Reed, chairman of the House Ways and Means Committee, justified tax breaks for the video game industry because they aid "the search for new products and new inventions upon which the future economic and military strength of our nation depends" (Kocieniewski, 2011). This book takes the position that there is wisdom in this statement.

Furthermore, based on certain metrics, video games are the dominant entertainment medium. Video games hold the title for "biggest entertainment release of all time." The multiplatform game *Grand Theft Auto V* made over 800 million dollars on the day it was released and made over one billion dollars by its second day on the market (Kain, 2013; Thier, 2013). This record was previously held by another video game, *Call of Duty: Black Ops 2* (Thier, 2013). To put this in perspective, the fastest selling book of all time was the seventh Harry Potter book, *Harry Potter and the Deathly Hallows*, which earned 330 million dollars on day one (Lea, 2007). Similarly, *Star Wars: The Force Awakens* was the fastest grossing movie of all time as it made 1 billion dollars in 12 days, edging out *Jurassic World,* which took 13 days (Cohen, 2015; Reuters, 2015). It took *Grand Theft Auto V* only two days to reach this benchmark. In summary, the top selling video games have outsold other top-selling forms of entertainment media by considerable amounts. Based on their earnings alone, major video game releases are considered the most successful form of entertainment, more so than traditional platforms such as books and movies. Of course, this feat must take into account that an average book or movie ticket costs much less than an average video game. *Grand Theft Auto V* was priced at 60 dollars per unit. The average movie ticket in 2015 when *Star Wars: The Force Awakens* was released was roughly eight dollars and new hardcover books were roughly priced at 30 dollars. A quick comparison reveals that about 17 million copies of *Grand Theft Auto V* were sold, 125 million tickets were sold over the 12-day period and 8.3 million copies of *Harry Potter and the Deathly Hallows* were sold. This demonstrates that many more tickets were sold to see *Star Wars: The Force Awakens* than were copies of *Grand Theft Auto V* and any claims related to video game sales should be interpreted through this lens. Generally, a video game is a larger investment than a movie ticket and thus we should expect to see fewer people consuming the product when looking at comparable figures. Regardless, video games are a huge part of contemporary society and merit attention as well as discussion.

Up to this point, the widespread importance of video games as compared to other media has been discussed, but what makes games different than other media has been neglected. The differences between video games and other media platforms are evident to even a casual observer but defining these differences is a bit more challenging and a source of disagreement in the research community.

Reeves and Read (2013), in their book *Total Engagement: How Games and Virtual Worlds Are Changing the Way People Work and Businesses Compete*, argued that there are a handful of typical ingredients for great games. They suggest the following:

1. Self-representation with avatars
2. 3D environments
3. Narrative context
4. Feedback
5. Reputations, ranks, and levels
6. Marketplaces and economies
7. Competition under explicit rules that are enforced
8. Teams
9. Parallel communication systems
10. Time pressure

Meanwhile, Jane McGonigal (2011), in *Reality Is Broken: Why Games Make Us Better and How They Can Change the World* suggested that the main traits of games are: goals, rules, feedback system, and voluntary participation.

Both books expanded on these concepts and made arguments for each. While all of the traits detailed by Reeves and Read are important, they did not argue that each trait was a necessity but rather these traits were typical of well-designed games. As a result, the Reeves and Read suggestions can be handled parsimoniously by focusing on critical elements of video games. For example, reputations, ranks, and levels can be subsumed by feedback mechanisms. Likewise, a marketplace and a narrative context are important but not present in some of the most popular video games in history such as *Tetris*.

As for McGonigal's listed traits, the attribute "voluntary participation" may be extraneous. Voluntary participation is an important variable to consider in video game consumption, however, there are many games such as educational video games or healthy video games that are not always played voluntarily but rather compulsorily. Further, much video game play in experimental research is compelled in a lab setting and therefore not voluntary in a traditional sense. Thus, it would be hard to qualify video games played in a lab setting and games used for therapy/education under McGonigal's definition. While there likely would be many psychological differences between players who use a video game voluntarily versus those who are compelled to play a video game, consideration of voluntary participation as a key element of games can be somewhat limiting.

In all, the current text argues that there are three key elements to video games: rules, interactivity/feedback, and self-presentation. Each of these will be detailed in the next portion of this book. In doing so, the book aims to provide a framework through which the reader can understand the effects of games within these key video game elements. In other words, rules, interactivity/feedback, and self-presentation all contribute to the effects of video games and to fully understand the effects, one must understand these concepts. This book takes the perspective that if video games can have negative impacts they can also have positive impacts. As a result, this book examines the positive and the negative effects of video games. The following section will examine some of the positive aspects of video games. Some issues covered will be: video games in education, video games and prosocial behaviors, as well as video games and mood management. The third section will examine some of the negative aspects of video games. Some of the issues covered will be: video games and violence, harassment behaviors in video games, diversity issues in video games, and substance use behaviors in video games. The conclusion predicts the future of video games within the context of these topics. Ultimately, the goal of this book is to provide a balanced and nuanced look at how video games play a complex role in our society as well as cultivate an understanding of how feedback, rules, and self-presentation factor into these issues.

WHO IS PLAYING VIDEO GAMES?

In each of my classes I perform a quick, nonscientific survey. I ask all of my students if they play video games. Invariably, only a handful of the students raise their hands. Then, I rephrase the question and ask who plays video games but I include popular mobile video games such as *Candy Crush Saga*, *Words with Friends*, and *2048*. In response to this question, nearly every student raises his or her hand. This short exercise demonstrates that even though almost all of the students play video games, many of them do not consider themselves video game players because they do not play certain video games.

I, with a handful of colleagues, decided to explore this phenomenon more formally (Rogers, Parrott, Barnard, & Dillman-Carpentier, 2012). In a survey, participants were asked what media platforms they think of when they hear the term "video game." Only 87 (of a possible 334 total responses) responses indicated a casual, web-browser game, or a mobile game on a smartphone/tablet. Meanwhile, respondents selected Xbox 159 times out of a possible 167, and PlayStation 142 times out of a possible 167. When asked to list the first four games that came to mind, only 10 of the games listed were exclusively internet browser or mobile device based. The rest were video games played on consoles or installed on computers.

These findings indicate that the term "video game" mainly applies to more traditional formats of video game play. This sample did not think of casual games as "video games." In the video game industry, both are considered video games but distinctions have been made between casual games and hardcore games (Paulding, 2008; Minkley, 2011). Casual video games are typically defined by low commitment and easily understood rules. Hardcore video games tend to be more complex and technologically advanced. Even though both are video games, the people in this sample tended to think of hardcore games more readily than casual games when they heard the term "video game." Importantly, this distinction seems to be subjective. *Minecraft* is popular with those typically considered casual and hardcore audiences because of the robust crafting systems and the huge open world (Albert, 2014). To summarize this study, many people play video games but do not often think of the games they are playing as "video games." Likewise, some video games might actually straddle the line between hardcore and casual appeal. This raises the question: Why does the distinction exist such that some video games count as video games but others do not? One possible explanation is that video game players are stigmatized.

Typically, video game players are negatively stereotyped (Griffiths, Davies, & Chappell, 2003; Marcotte, 2015). Content on popular television networks such as Comedy Central and NBC might be perpetuating stereotypes of those who play video games. For example, a recent episode of *Law and Order: Special Victims Unit* featured a husband and wife who were suspected of pedophilia and child abuse. When police entered the couple's home, they refused to leave the television set because they were almost to the end of a video game that they had been playing for days. The couple appeared filthy, morbidly obese, disheveled, and completely divorced from reality because of the video game. Such a portrayal is not far removed from other popular media portrayals. In an episode called "Make Love, Not Warcraft," the main characters of the animated program *South Park* become obsessed with online gaming. Soon the characters became glued to their computer monitors, sitting among empty soda bottles and potato chip bags, unable to step away from the game. The characters become unhealthily overweight, acne covered their faces, and grease filled their hair because they had not showered in so long. Lastly, in *The Big Bang Theory*, actor Jim Parsons has won four Emmys for his portrayal of a smart, yet socially inept, and possibly mentally ill character who loves video games. Despite the humor of *South Park* and *The Big Bang Theory*, such content may serve to reinforce the negative stereotype of video game players.

The negative stereotype of video game players is likely also informed by news media stories that link video game play to perpetrators of violent acts. Eric Harris and Dylan Klebold, the shooters in the Columbine massacre were players of the video game *Doom* (Brown, 1999). There were even rumors that the two recreated the halls of their high school within the game space in order to practice their rampage. Anders Behring Breivik, perpetrator of the massacre of over 80 people in Norway was reported to be a fan of the first-person shooter series *Call of Duty* (Pidd, 2012). Allegedly, he even familiar-ized himself with the equipment used in his massacre through video game play. Adam Lanza killed 20 children and six adult staff members at Sandy Hook Elementary School and was an avid video game player (Ferguson, 2013). Elliot Rodger, who went on a killing spree in Isla Vista, California, was a regular player of *World of Warcraft* (Nagourney, Cieply, Feuer, & Lovett, 2014). In each instance, the news story indicated that a video game player committed a violent act, thereby tying video game play to acts of violence directly or indirectly. These sorts of portrayals may contribute to the negative stereotype of video game players.

According to the process-based conceptual model proposed by Link and Phelan (2001), once video game players are labeled and stereotyped, they can become stigmatized and discriminated against. An example may help illus-trate the process. Steve, a college student, loves the first-person shooter game *Call of Duty: Modern Warfare*, which he plays most weeknights with old high school friends who are scattered across the United States. When the fall semester begins, Steve wears his new *Modern Warfare* T-shirt to history class on the first day. When another student walks into the classroom, he or she may spot the T-shirt and label Steve as a video game player. This label activates stereotypes about video game players, which may influence the student's decision whether he or she should sit by Steve.

Needless to say, media portrayals of video game players do not provide a complete picture. The demographic makeup of who is playing video games is much more widely varied than such stereotypes imply. Here are a few facts to help illustrate this point from the Entertainment Software Association (2014) and Griffiths et al. (2003):

- Forty-eight percent of video game players are women.
- The average video game player is in his or her 30s, not in his or her teens.
- The white socially withdrawn adolescent male stereotype disregards a large section of the gaming population.

Thus, there is incongruence between who is perceived to be playing video games and who is actually playing them. While describing who plays video games is important for the exposition of this book, the stigmatization of video game players, itself, is a social issue. When video game players are stigmatized they are discriminated against, devalued, and enjoy a lower quality of life (Jacoby, Snape, & Baker, 2005). Meanwhile, research shows video games can benefit players by increasing motivation, enhancing learning, and encouraging meaningful social interactions, but anti-video game bias may prevent video games from being used to their full potential (McGonigal, 2011; Reeves & Read, 2009). In other words, the benefits of video games will not be fully employed until the stigmatization of video game players has dissipated.

To explore the stigmatization of video game players, a few colleagues and I surveyed 167 undergraduate students at a southeastern university (Rogers et al., 2012). Using a method adapted from Olmstead and Durham (1976), respondents ranked how well adjectives described a few different groups: "an average person"; "yourself"; "a doctor"; "a mental patient"; and "a video game player."

This study revealed video game players were perceived to be significantly different than each of the other four groups, such that video game players were viewed more negatively when compared to the respondent ("yourself"), the average person, and a doctor, but more positively than mental patients. However, it is worth pointing out that the mean difference between video game players and mental patients was the smallest, potentially suggesting that those two groups were the most similar. Further analysis revealed that video game players were regarded as more worthless, weak, violent, anti-social, and unpopular than all groups except for mental patients, which were not significantly different. Video game players were also thought to be significantly more dirty, lazy, overweight, immature, nerdy, and unattractive than all other groups, including mental patients. All groups were regarded as less dependent on others and less abnormal than video game players—except for mental patients, who were regarded as more dependent on others and more abnormal. Lastly, video game players were thought to be more predictable than mental patients and less predictable than doctors. There were no differences between video game players and the respondent ("yourself") or between video game players and an average person on these dimensions.

In summary, video game players were viewed more negatively than each group, with the exception of mental patients. However, the difference between mental patients and video game players was the smallest, suggesting that video game players were considered to be more similar to mental patients than to an average person, a doctor, or the respondent ("yourself"). Stigma issues regarding mental illness notwithstanding, this indicates where video game players are valued in a social hierarchy. Furthermore, this suggests an "us" and "them" mentality when it comes to video game players and others. People prefer to distance themselves from video game players. Taking cues from media portrayals of video game players, these results indicate that the negative video game player stereotype is indeed salient and accessible. The characteristics of a video game player shown here are comparable to ones portrayed in the aforementioned episodes of *Law and Order: SVU* and *South Park*, as well as in various news stories. This appears to be the case in spite of the inaccuracy of the stereotype and the widespread use of video games.

Regardless of the negative stereotype of video game players, who is playing video games? Almost everyone. The next chapter will explore the three key elements of video games: rules, interactivity/feedback, and self-presentation.

REFERENCES

Albert, B. (2014). Building worlds. *IGN.com.* http://www.ign.com/articles/2014/01/24/minecraft-review-2

Brown, J. (1999). Doom, Quake and mass murder. *Salon.* http://www.salon.com/1999/04/23/gamers/

Cohen, S. (2015). *Force Awakens* becomes fastest movie to $1 billion. *Finance.Yahoo.com.* http://finance.yahoo.com/news/force-awakens-becomes-fastest-movie-162407895.html

Entertainment Software Association (2014). Essential facts. *Esa.*org. http://www.theesa.com/wp-content/uploads/2014/10/ESA_EF_2014.pdf

Ferguson, C. (2013). Adam Lanza's motive a mystery in Sandy Hook killings. *CNN.* http://edition.cnn.com/2013/11/27/opinion/ferguson-sandy-hook/

Griffiths, M. D., Davies, M. O., & Chappell, D. (2003). Breaking the stereotype: The case of online gaming. *Cyberpsychology & Behavior, 6*(1), 81–91.

Jacoby, A., Snape, D., & Baker, G. A. (2005). Epilepsy and social identity: the stigma of a chronic neurological disorder. *The Lancet Neurology, 4*(3), 171–178.

Kain, E. (2013). *Grand Theft Auto V* crosses $1B in sales, biggest entertainment launch in history. *Forbes.com.* http://www.forbes.com/sites/erikkain/2013/09/20/grand-theft-auto-v-crosses-1b-in-sales-biggest-entertainment-launch-in-history/

Kocieniewski, D. (2011). Rich tax breaks bolster makers of video games. *NYTimes.com.* http://www.nytimes.com/2011/09/11/technology/rich-tax-breaks-bolster-video-game-makers.html?pagewanted=all&_r=0

Lea, K. (2007). Potter magic smashes publishing records. *TheGuardian.com.* http://www.theguardian.com/books/2007/jul/23/harrypotter.jkjoannekathleenrowling1

Link, B. G., and Phelan, J. C. (2001) Conceptualizing Stigma. *Annual Review of Sociology,* 363–385.

Marcotte, A. (2015). Teen girls love video games, but they're really quiet about it. *Slate.com.* http://www.slate.com/blogs/xx_factor/2015/08/18/teen_girls_play_video_games_but_they_minimize_their_contact_with_other_players.html?wpsrc=sh_all_dt_tw_bot

McGonigal, J. (2011). *Reality is broken: Why games make us better and how they can change the world.* Penguin.

Minkley, J. (2011). Miyamoto: Wii created core/casual split. *Eurogamer.net.* http://www.eurogamer.net/articles/2011-06-08-miyamoto-wii-created-core-casual-split

Nagourney, A., Cieply, M., Feuer, A., & Lovett, I. (2014). Before brief, deadly spree, trouble since age 8. *NYTimes.com.* http://www.nytimes.com/2014/06/02/us/elliot-rodger-killings-in-california-followed-years-of-withdrawal.html?_r=0

Olmsted, D. W., & Durham, K. (1976). Stability of mental health attitudes: A semantic differential study. *Journal of Health and Social Behavior*, *17*, 35–44.

Paulding, J. (2008). Casual vs. hardcore games. *G4TV.com*. http://www.g4tv.com/thefeed/blog/post/683070/casual-vs-hardcore-games/

Pidd, H. (2012). Anders Breivik "trained" for shooting attacks by playing *Call of Duty*. *The Guardian*. http://www.guardian.co.uk/world/2012/apr/19/anders-breivik-call-of-duty

Reeves, B., & Read, J. L. (2009). *Total engagement: Using games and virtual worlds to changes the way people work and businesses compete*. Boston: Harvard University Press.

Reeves, B., & Read, J. L. (2013). *Total engagement: How games and virtual worlds are changing the way people work and businesses compete*. Boston: Harvard Business Press.

Reuters (2015). *Jurassic World* set to become fastest film to gross $1 billion. *Yahoo.com*. https://www.yahoo.com/tv/s/jurassic-world-set-become-fastest-film-gross-1-205159590--finance.html?nf=1

Rogers, R., Parrott, S., Barnard, L., & Dillman-Carpentier, F. (2012). *Video games and undergraduates: Methodological considerations for video game studies using an undergraduate sample*. Unpublished manuscript, Department of Mass Communication, University of North Carolina, Chapel Hill, NC.

Takahashi, D. (2014). Video game retail sales slipped in 2013 as gamers prepped for new consoles. *Venturebeat.com*. http://venturebeat.com/2014/01/16/2013-was-a-transition-year-for-video-game-industry-retail-sales/

Thier, D. (2013). *GTA 5* sells $800 million in one day. *Forbes.com*. http://www.forbes.com/sites/davidthier/2013/09/18/gta-5-sells-800-million-in-one-day/

I

Overview

Chapter One

Three Key Elements of Video Games

Rules, Interactivity/Feedback, and Self-Presentation

RULES

One of the biggest differences between video games and other media formats is that video games have rules. Broadly, rules are principles intended to guide behavior. Within video games, rules can be understood as the laws that govern the game space or the parameters that a player must function within to master the game. Even the game's industry has its own rules: the Entertainment Software Rating Board (ESRB) issues a rating for roughly 1,000 games each year (ESRB.org, 2014b). The stated purpose of the ESRB is to enhance customer literacy and to inform consumers/parents as to what content is included in certain games (ESRB.org, 2014a). The system is voluntary and self-policing.

The study of games broadly, or ludology, has described rules as a game's structure through elements predefined by a content creator (Frasca, 2003). In the case of video games, the individuals who program the video game dictate the rules; and rules allow the programmer to determine what the game experience will be. From a video game player's perspective, rules are a component of video game design that allow users to understand the fundamental structure underpinning the game (Apperley, 2006). Salen and Zimmerman (2004) describe three levels of rules:

1. Constitutive rules refer to the mathematical foundations that dictate the logic of a game. This relates to the programming of a game on the most fundamental level or the code. The way in which a virtual space is coded determines the laws of that space (Lessig, 2006).

3

2. Operational rules communicate, to the user through instructions, how the game is played. Typically, these are an interpretation of the constituative rules, but presented in a way that the player can understand them, perhaps through tutorials or text boxes.
3. Implicit rules are not necessarily formal rules dictated by the video game's design, but are more related to game etiquette. For example, it may not be officially against the rules of *Halo* to shoot your teammates or otherwise engage in unsportsmanlike behaviors but many who play video games expect that other players will be good teammates and work toward the shared goal of winning the match.

Juul (2011) states that video games generally *depend* on clearly defined, easy to understand rules. Also, rules are both limitations and affordances in video games. In other words, rules determine what players cannot do but also what they *can* do. In doing so, rules define the game experience and, according to Juul (2011), rules should do the following:

1. Provide understandable guidelines.
2. Create a "machine" that responds to player action.
3. Create challenges derived from seeking certain outcomes.
4. Interact with the player.
5. Help players learn how to improve/sharpen skills.
6. Emphasize different challenges in the video game and distinguish the game from other video games.

It is important to note, other forms of media do not have "rules" in the same manner. Certainly, a movie can have rules within the narrative (consider the time travel rules in *Back to the Future*) but these rules inform and do not *dictate* the audience's experience with the content like a video game's rules do. A more appropriate comparison would be that we are expected to be quiet in a movie theatre and not use our phones. However, this only covers Salen and Zimmerman's (2004) notion of implicit rules and does not address constituative or operational rules created by the game's content producers. Further, there are constraints to media formats that might be confused with rules. For example, you cannot rewind a movie while seeing it in the theater; this is not a rule per se but a general characteristic of the experience with that medium.

Game studies literature expands on the difference between games and other media such that narrative aspects of video games are often conflated with design aspects of games (Frasca, 2003). Apperley (2006) offers an example in terms of the *Dungeons and Dragons* franchise. Based closely on fantasy literature, *Dungeons and Dragons* games differ from fantasy literature because they simulate being inside the story. Implementing certain rules and giving the player limitations/affordances are designed to simulate a fantasy adventure thereby placing a player inside the story. Whereas a fantasy novel lacks these traits, *Dungeons and Dragons* games use rules to create an authentic experience inspired by fantasy literature (Apperley, 2006).

In that vein, a game can be understood as a sum of its rules (Parlett, 1999). Game genres are often defined based on their rules. Simulators emphasize authenticity in their rules, action games emphasize player performance in their rules, horror games implement rules that make the player feel helpless to increase feelings of terror (Apperley, 2006). Consider the horror game *Dead Space*. In many video games, maps and inventory items are available in a menu when the game is paused or when the player stops game play. In *Dead Space*, all map viewing and inventory management is done while the game progresses in real time. In other words, the player cannot stop the game to perform these tasks. This slight tweak to the rules creates a heightened sense of danger for the player as he or she can be attacked while performing tasks that are safe in other games. Similarly, the game designers of *Dead Space* at Visceral Games made resources scarce, forcing the players to make decisions that impact the likelihood of their survival (Haynes, 2008). The sequels, *Dead Space 2* and *3*, offer modes that only allow three save checkpoints or death results in the game starting from the beginning. Again, the rules in these modes enhance the feelings of risk and ultimately, the horror/dread felt by the player.

Even the earliest video games were defined by their rules. Arcade games were typically coin-operated, meaning the player purchased one round of play for each coin, usually a quarter, he or she inserted into the machine. Thus, the games were designed in such a way that the rules could not be mastered on the first attempt. Most arcade games took a few attempts to learn the rules and therefore, the rules were used to generate more revenue per player. For example, *Donkey Kong* offers virtually no training to the player. During the first round of play, the player might not understand that he or she has to press up to climb a ladder. This lack of knowledge results in loss of a life in the game. On the second attempt, the player might not realize that the barrels hurtling toward him or her are following different patterns and lose another life in the game. All of a sudden the player has one life remaining in a game designed to be very difficult and unforgiving. The player is forced, by the rules, to insert another quarter to play more and learn more about the game.

Even games within the same genre become distinct experiences because of the use of different rules. Two of the most popular first person shooter franchises, *Halo* and *Call of Duty* are ostensibly, very similar games. Both are first-person shooters that feature soldiers in a theater of war where players aim down the sights of various weapons to eliminate enemies. Due to their similarities and success, the franchises are often compared but nuances in the rules distinguish the games from one another (see Cooper & Veloria, 2012; Legarie, 2012). For example, *Halo* allows for the use of vehicles and cooperative play that *Call of Duty* does not offer. Meanwhile, *Call of Duty* offers a much more robust competitive multiplayer suite with a wider variety of game modes. Web article comments and discussion boards demonstrate just how different these games feel to their respective fans. While many of these comments relate to graphics and narrative, others relate to games' rules. One player says of *Halo* "Custom games gave people so much control" and another player in defense of *Call of Duty* (COD) says, "There were good weapons in every COD, but contrary to complainers' opinions, very few were OP (overpowered). The only weapon that did too much damage was the 1887 and they nerfed (made weaker) it when everyone was complaining." In both cases, players are referring to intricacies of the rules of the video games.

The importance of rules in games has ushered in the concept of the magic circle. Magic circles are isolated spots where special rules, or lack of rules, pertain (Huizinga, 2014). Within the magic circle, certain behaviors might be allowed or encouraged that are not allowed or encouraged outside of the magic circle (Jenkins, 2006). When playing a game, the laws of the game space take precedence and real world laws do not necessarily apply to the game space (Fairfield, 2009). Another way to think of the magic circle is in terms of consent or a social contract (Fairfield, 2009; Montola, 2005). This means that the users agree to the terms and conditions, or the rules, of play. For an illustrative example, consider a tackle in a game of football. This action is permitted and encouraged while in the game space. However, the same action outside of a game, and therefore outside of the magic circle, could result in an arrest and assault charges. Similarly, in many video games the object of the game is to kill other players. This is often rewarded in games but would be punished severely outside of them.

While many actions are permitted in games that are illegal outside of the game space, not everything is permitted in a game. When an action in a video game defies the magic circle, this can translate into legal action. For example, two *Runescape* players forced a third player to log into his account and transfer two valuable items (an amulet and a mask) to another account. This was considered theft due to the fact that the mask and amulet had monetary value outside of the game (Telegraph.co.uk, 2012). Similarly, a man and woman were married in a virtual world game called *Maple Story*, not married in the offline world. Feeling spurned after an abrupt online divorce, the woman logged into her online husband's account and deleted his avatar. According to police, she killed his online persona and faced up to five years in prison (Katz, 2008). For another example, in the computer game *Lambda-Moo* one player, known as Mr. Bungle, used a program that forced other users' characters to engage in sexual actions without consent (Dibbell, 1993). This transgression resulted in the *LambdaMoo* community forming a tribunal to decide how to punish Mr. Bungle. In each of these cases, the magic circle was broken. Rules that were in place were breached and there was a major infraction in the game and in some cases, outside of the game. In the first two examples, legal action was taken. In the Mr. Bungle example, the game adjusted its rules to account for this behavior. For a more recent example, a *World of Warcraft* player named Mike Weatherley had a virtual sword stolen from him (Buist, 2014). In response to this incident, the United Kingdom's chief adviser on intellectual property said that virtual theft should be treated in the same fashion as real world theft.

While some scholars have challenged the usefulness of the magic circle (see Consalvo, 2005, 2009; Fairfield, 2009), the examples above and the robust debate of the magic circle highlight the critical role of rules in the domain of video games. Given the particular salience of rules in video games, a discussion on the effects of video games should do so with special attention to rules. Notably, video game rules are often discussed alongside video game feedback (McGonigal 2011; Reeves & Read, 2013). While the topics are closely related, for the sake of clarity this book suggests that rules are more appropriately discussed as a distinct concept from feedback, which is examined next.

INTERACTIVITY/FEEDBACK

Another key difference between video games and other media formats is interactivity. Video games are inherently interactive (Grodal, 2000) and much has been made of the power of interactivity in a variety of disciplines as well as the popular press (Gallaga, 2012; LeFebvre, 2012; Reeves, 2012); so much so that interactivity could be considered a buzzword in modern society, and with good reason. High levels of interactivity can be linked to positive attitudes toward content and better memory of content (Ariely 2000; Sundar & Kim, 2005; Teo, Oh, Liu, & Wei, 2003). From the perspective of a content producer, creating memorable and likeable content is a worthwhile endeavor.

While the impact of interactivity is generally agreed upon, what constitutes interactivity has been a topic of much deliberation. Interactivity has been defined in the following ways:

1. "A measure of a media's potential ability to let the user exert an influence on the content and/or form of the mediated communication" (Jensen, 1998, p. 201). This conceptualization defines interactivity as user control. This is then parsed into four subcategories. On the most basic level, interactive content lets the user choose his or her information in one-way communication like clicking on a news story from

CNN.com. The next category allows users to choose preproduced content in a two-way communication system such that users are choosing to respond to the system from preset dialogue options. Third, the user can input his or her own information as a response to the system. Lastly, users can input their information and the system adapts to the input. The last category most accurately describes the interactivity found in video games.

2. Similarly to Jensen's conceptualization, Ariely (2000) discusses interactivity in terms of user control of information flow. Traditional media offers little control of information flow such that the flow of a television news program is largely out of the audience members' control. Notably, while new media technology *can* offer more control to users, it does not necessarily do so. When a user can control information flow, he or she can access pertinent information when it is relevant. Dynamic heterogeneity describes the changing need for information during an interactive information gathering session (Ariely, 2000). In other words, a user has control over the content and can fluidly generate and test the hypothesis in which he or she is interested during the process.

3. A third conceptualization of interactivity argues that "increased interactivity simply translates to an interface's capacity for conducting a dialogue or information exchange between users and the interface" (Sundar, Kalyanaraman, & Brown, 2003, p. 3). Under this definition, an interface is more interactive when it has more technological features that allow for dialogue. This is known as the functional view of interactivity.

4. In contrast with the functional view, the contingency view of interactivity states that interactivity is "a process involving users, media, and messages, with an emphasis on how messages relate to one another" (Sundar et al., 2003, p. 34). This means that a user and an interface exchange messages and the messages logically follow one another such that they are contingent upon one another.

5. Lastly, Bucy (2004) argues that interactivity is not a product feature at all, but rather, a user's perception of the interface. Essentially, interactivity is something that a person feels or does not feel when using a technological interface. Bucy argues that only when we have a larger body of knowledge of how interactivity works can we start to adequately assess it as a concept.

This list is not exhaustive by any means but it does highlight considerable differences between conceptualizations of interactivity. Despite the lack of consensus, most agree that video games are interactive. Within the domain of video games, interactivity can be manifested in (Reeves & Read, 2013):

- Speed (the time it takes for a game to respond to input)
- Mapping (the match between virtual actions and natural actions in the physical world, e.g., action mimicked: pulling a trigger to simulate firing a gun or swinging a controller to simulate swinging a knife vs. action not mimicked: pressing a button to grapple with an enemy)
- Range (the number of different responses as a result of input)

Based on these descriptions, a game like *Temple Run*, which forces the player forward while the player reacts to oncoming obstacles, would not be very interactive. Meanwhile, a game like *Grand Theft Auto V*, that exhibits more of a "sandbox" style of play, in which players can choose how they want to play, where they want to go, and what tools they use in the process, would be highly interactive. On top of that, interactivity can shift within a game such that certain moments are more interactive than others. For example, in one game a player may experience a "cut-scene" or a short cinematic sequence, which allows for no interactivity. After that, he or she may enter a game play sequence that allows for a full range of control (explore where one prefers, change equipment, and controller layouts). Then he or she may enter an "on-rails" sequence or a moment like *Temple Run*, which pushes the player forward automatically while he or she reacts to obstacles.

To illustrate this complexity, a content analysis of video games that included a series of measures for interactivity was performed (Rogers, 2013). The top 20 games, by number sold between 2010–2012, were identified by the sales figures on vgchartz.com, a source cited by the *New York Times* (Muskus, 2008), *Forbes* (Noer, 2008) and the *BBC* (Reed, 2008). A similar sampling strategy has been used in previous video game content analyses (Dietz, 1998; Ivory, Williams, Martins, & Consalvo, 2009; Martins, Williams, & Harrison, 2008; Thompson & Haninger, 2001; Thompson, Tepichin, & Haninger, 2006). Each game was played for 30 minutes from the start screen. The start screen was identified as the screen where the player first initializes a playable game mode (typically after developer and publisher company logos and accompanied by a menu and a "press start" or "press a button" instruction). If a game featured multiple game modes, the default game mode was chosen. The default game mode was identified as whichever mode was pre-selected by the game (cursor was already on the mode, the mode was already highlighted, identified as the "main mode," single player mode, campaign mode).

For each game, each occurrence of violence, or physical attack between characters in a video game intended to cause harm, was coded (Thompson & Haninger, 2001). The number of occurrences in each game was coded as well as the duration (in seconds). Violence was then coded as realistic violence (violence that could be replicated in the world not mediated by video games [e.g., gun or knife violence]), fantasy violence (fantastic elements that are

integral to the violence such as magic, paranormal activity, or alien weapon-
ry), or comic violence (cartoon style violence that shows abstract representations of violence like flashing objects or stars to represent dazed characters).
Then, the presence of gore was noted: if blood was present the occurrence
was considered gory, if no blood was present then it was considered not gory.
These categories were based on current video game rating system classifica-
tions (ESRB.org, 2015). The direction of the violence was also coded, that is:
was the player on the receiving end of the violence, was the player inflicting
the violence, and was violence exchanged between the player and others, or
did the violence not include the player?

Each occurrence of violence was coded for user control. First, the study
noted if the player had no control over the violence (it took place between
two non-player characters in the background or in a narrative sequence) or if
the violence involved player control. If an occurrence was out of the players'
control then coders noted if the occurrence was in a narrative sequence or a
gameplay sequence. Video game violence can take place in narrative sequences (often called cut-scenes that cut away from game play to advance
the plot) in which the player has no control at all (over violence, actions,
view, etc.). In game play sequences players have some degree of control (full
or limited range). If the violence was under the players' control then other
aspects were coded.

The occurrence of violence was also coded for valence. In other words,
was the consequence of the violence portrayed as positive, negative, or neutral? Positive portrayals of violence helped players reach in-game goals.
Negative portrayals hindered players from reaching in-game goals. Neutral
acts of violence had no bearing on the player's achievement of in-game
goals. Importantly, this did not take into account any external offline-world
normative values of violence such that violence can be viewed as socially
undesirable.

On the most fundamental level, this sample included more than twice as
much violence that was under the users' control (200) than not (81). As such,
interactive violence was more common than non-interactive violence under
certain conceptualizations. However, it may come as a surprise that over a
quarter of the occurrences of violence were not interactive. This is an important finding and suggests how video game content (violence) can vary by
interactivity. One might assume that all video game content is interactive but
this assumption would be inaccurate.

Moreover, user controlled violence in video games varied within other
attributes important to conceptualizations of interactivity. Sixty-one of the
occurrences mimicked the actual violent action such as firing a gun by pulling a trigger. It is possible that mimicking a violent action with one's own
body would result in more arousal than violence that does not mimic the
action. Likewise, performing an action results in better recall of the action

than watching someone perform an action (Engelkamp & Zimmer, 2002; Old & Naveh-Benjamin, 2008). This is worth considering in light of the influx of motion-controlled video game interfaces like the Nintendo Wii, the PlayStation Move, and the Xbox Kinect.

Fifty-five of the instances of violence were automated such that the player initiated the violence but then relinquished control to an animation sequence. Players had flexible options (dynamic heterogeneity) in 179 occurrences and no flexibility in 21 occurrences. This flexibility is what makes interactive content more influential (Ariely, 2000). Thus, violent content should be more influential when it allows for flexible options than when the violence is automated. In summary, not only does interactivity vary in a game but the degree of interactivity changes such that some content is more interactive than others.

Lastly, content in this study tended to have different characteristics when it was user controlled as opposed to when it was not. The mean duration of controlled violence was 31.87 seconds ($SD = 42.81$) while the mean duration of non-controlled violence was 22.88 seconds ($SD = 62.82$). Controlled violence also tended to be more realistic (30.50%) than not (19.80%) but comical violence was most common for both controlled (46.50%) and not controlled violence (60.50%). Moreover, controlled violence was gory (34%) more often than non-controlled violence (9.90%). This is noteworthy because graphic violence can serve as a prime for players and increase aggression of players (Sherry, 2001). Non-controlled violence was also most commonly portrayed as neutral (54.30%) and controlled violence was most commonly portrayed as positive (81.50%). According to social cognitive theory, individuals are more likely to mimic a behavior when it is portrayed with positive outcomes than when the behavior is portrayed to have a negative outcome (Bandura, 2002). Thus, controlled violence is more likely to be emulated than non-controlled violence because the player acts it out and it is portrayed with positive consequences. Non-controlled violence, most commonly, was directed toward the player (50.60%) or did not involve the player (43.20%) while controlled violence was most commonly an exchange between the player and another game character (90.50%).

The social implications of the above findings notwithstanding, interactivity in video games is extremely complex. This, in conjunction with the lack of consensus on what constitutes interactivity, makes it difficult to examine interactivity as a key element of video games. As a result, it is additionally useful to examine video games using a concept closely related to interactivity: feedback.

Norbert Wiener (1961, p. 6), who is credited with formalizing the concept of feedback, describes it as follows:

When we desire a motion to follow a given pattern, the difference between this
pattern and the actually performed motion is used as a new input to cause the
part regulated to move in such a way as to bring its motion closer to that given
by the pattern.

With foundations in engineering (Mindell, 2003), feedback has been applied
to many other domains such as cybernetics, ecology, and human behavior
(Bowlby, 1982; Miller, Galanter, & Pribram, 1960; Goetz, 2011; Senge,
1990). Accordingly, Wiener's definition has been adapted and updated, but
in most scenarios, feedback generally describes the same process: an individual is given information about a previous behavior and this information is
intended to improve performance on a subsequent behavior (Hattie & Timperley, 2007; Hawkins, Kreuter, Resnicow, Fishbein, & Dijkstra, 2008, p.
459; Winne & Butler, 1994, p. 5740). Terms like "feedback loop" (Carver &
Scheier, 2001; Ramaprasad, 1983) and "feedback intervention" (Glanz,
Schoenfeld, & Steffen, 2010; Haug, Meyer, Ulbricht, Gross, & Rumpf, John,
2010; Kluger & DeNisi, 1996; Ruiter, Werrij, & de Vries, 2010) are commonly used and refer to the same overarching concept.

More specifically, feedback is the comparison of values within a circular
system in which components of the system influence one another (Ashby,
1956). Under this conceptualization, feedback consists of four parts: input,
reference value, comparator, and output (Ashby, 1956; Goetz, 2011; Carver
& Scheier, 2001). Input refers to how information enters/begins a feedback
loop. This information can be any sort of measure, like: performance on an
exam, money spent over a week, amount of electricity used per resident, etc.
(Ramaprasad, 1983). A reference value is a goal or a standard. The reference
value serves as a comparison standard to the input value. The comparison can
have one of two possible results; the values are the same or the values are
different. The output is the information regarding the discrepancy (or lack
thereof) between the input value and the reference value. These four components create a feedback loop or feedback system. In summary, the input value
is compared to the reference value and the output is fed back toward the input
where it should influence subsequent input values. For an illustrative example of a feedback loop, imagine a person taking a road trip on a tight budget.
The actual money spent represents the input value. The proposed budget
represents the reference value. A comparison shows how much more or less
the person spent than the budget allowed. This information informs the person so he or she knows if more or less money can be spent on his or her next
road trip to remain on budget.

Feedback has assumed many shapes: grades in classrooms that help students pursue educational goals (Hattie & Timperley, 2007), reciprocity in
counseling sessions that help patients achieve therapeutic goals (Thiemann &
Goldstein, 2001), annual employee evaluations that help companies/employ-

ees provide better products/services (Connellan & Zemke, 1993), and automobile speedometers that provide information to help motorists drive legally and safely (Goetz, 2011). Even the perception of feedback (i.e., feedback that does not necessarily reflect exact performance) is effective in influencing individual performance or perceptions of performance (Beedie, Lane, & Wilson, 2012; Gu, Zhong, & Page-Gould, 2013; Reinecke et al., 2012). For example, in one study, participants were told they had performed well or performed poorly regardless of their actual performance and this false feedback altered feelings of competence and autonomy (Reinecke et al., 2012). This finding, that even the perception of feedback alters psychological variables, highlights that feedback is an authoritative form of interactivity that should be obeyed if one wants to achieve certain goals.

The loop conceptualization of feedback is perhaps even more closely related to conceptualizations of interactivity (Kalyanaraman & Sundar, 2008; Sundar, Kalyanaraman, & Brown, 2003) such that feedback can be understood as goal-oriented interactivity, a notion central to the overall experience with video game content. It is this book's position that feedback fundamentally describes a dialogue between the user and the interface. In video game environments, player input is assessed by the game and the game, in turn, conveys information back to the player, communicating progress (or lack of progress) toward the game goal. Then, the player's next input should incorporate this newly acquired information and the cycle repeats. In essence, the experience of playing a game relies on feedback. In video games, it is generally accepted that feedback, like a scoring mechanism, is used to enhance player performance by helping players reach game goals (Bowman, 1982; Lee, Luchini, Michael, Norris, & Soloway, 2004). In video game environments, providing aural and visual rewards like flashing lights and mechanical ringing tones (Lim et al., 2012; Wood, Griffiths, Chappell, & Davies, 2004), and tactile sensations (Ahn, 2011) offer feedback.

This book argues that video games can be optimal delivery systems for feedback because they allow for feedback that is immediate, continuously displayed, automatically delivered to the player, and presented in a controlled environment. Juul (2010) used the video game *Guitar Hero* as an example of effective video game feedback. In *Guitar Hero*, when players are performing well, a recognizable songs plays, the screen lights up with bonuses, and the crowd cheers with delight. When players are performing poorly, harsh, out-of-tune notes interrupt the song, the screen changes to an ominous color, and the crowd boos the performance. But *Guitar Hero* only represents one example of video game feedback. Even older games, like *Pac-Man*, use feedback. Each ghost Pac-Man eats shows a point value, which is then added to the player's total score. On top of the visual satisfaction of seeing the score increase, the game uses audio cues to denote certain behaviors. Pac-Man's iconic "wakka wakka" indicates the game is still going and points are still being accrued. Alternately, the player hears a lowering droop when Pac-Man dies, indicating a setback to the game goal. It is no coincidence that *Pac-Man* and *Guitar Hero* were wildly popular when they were first released.

In conclusion, video games are interactive by almost any characterization but interactivity is difficult to define. As a result, feedback is a valuable framework for examining video games. Video games can be extremely effective at delivering feedback but more importantly, the act of video game play would not be possible without feedback. Accordingly, video games are capable of shaping behaviors as well as attitudes toward behaviors through feedback and that has a considerable bearing on the effects of video games.

SELF-PRESENTATION

The last major difference between video games and other forms of traditional media is self-presentation. According to Baumeister (1998), the self can be a tool for interacting with others. In the context of video games, players are often required to present themselves; in virtually every video game, the player is represented somehow within the game space. This representation is called an avatar. However, the types of avatars used in video games are as diverse as the types of games themselves. In a video game like *The Sims 4* players can alter their avatar's facial features, body shape, skin tone, hair style, clothing, makeup, tattoos, movements, voices, personality traits, and behaviors. In *The Sims 4*, players have a large degree of flexibility in terms of how they choose to present themselves. In a game like *Call of Duty: Black Ops*, players have many fewer options but they still can choose how their characters appear on screen as well as the skills of that character. For example, players can select their equipment, their logo, and their clothing. The logo and clothing are only aesthetic but the equipment selected for the avatar alters the characters' abilities. In a video game like *Super Mario Kart*, players have even fewer options such that players have to choose from a bank of predetermined characters. For example, one player might select Mario instead of Bowser and these characters look different but also have different strengths/weaknesses. Regardless, in each instance, players are allowed to choose how they present themselves to other players and other characters in the game.

Importantly, all video games do not allow players to customize an avatar or select an avatar from a bank of characters. In these video games, players are represented by a standardized or default character. For example, in the video game *Alan Wake* every player uses the eponymous character when he or she experiences the game. Meanwhile, commonly in strategy video games, players are not represented by a character at all but rather by a reticle, or a series of lines that can be used to highlight and select things on screen. In the video game *XCOM: Enemy Unknown* players control a team of soldiers rather than one individual character. As a result, players use a selection tool from a "God's eye view" to move these characters around in the game. Even in these instances players might alter character names and play style, thus presenting themselves. In this way, even when a video game assigns an avatar to the players, players choose how to present themselves within the game space.

Baumeister (1998) provides scenarios of self-presentation that illuminate how a player might choose to present him or herself in a video game. People often present themselves in order to gain rewards or to ingratiate themselves to others. In other instances, people present themselves so they seem intimidating to scare off competition or people try to seem needy so others are more willing to help them. These forms of self-presentation are possible in the physical world but are even more easily achieved in virtual environments. Because of the anonymous and mediated nature of video games, it is much easier for players to present themselves in a desired manner than it is in the physical world.

Self-presentation is more flexible in virtual environments than in physical environments because certain things are possible in virtual environments that are not in the physical world (Leung, Virwaney, Lin, Armstrong, & Dubbelboer, 2013; Loomis, Blascovich, & Beall, 1999). This is known as transformed social interaction (TSI) (Bailenson, Beall, Loomis, Blascovich, & Turk, 2004). TSI is a paradigm that highlights a disconnection between human characteristics and representation in a virtual environment. In other words, TSI details a decoupling of the virtual world and the physical world such that the self presented in a video game is not bound by the laws of the physical world and thus can be manipulated and altered in unique ways (Bailenson & Yee, 2006). Within TSI, self-transformation specifically refers to the fact that in virtual environments people can transform themselves with avatars (Bailenson et al., 2004). Self-transformation, in other disciplines, suggests a change in an individual's values or identity (Carpenter, Brockopp, & Andrykowski, 1999; Lancaster & Palframan, 2009; Warren, 1992). An avatar can demonstrate emotions, expressions, appearances, etc. that may not actually reflect the user's current state. If someone tends to turn red when embarrassed, he or she can insulate him or herself from that with an avatar that does not blush. For a more extreme example, a video game player can experience the virtual world as a race that is incongruent with his or her race in the physical world (Bailenson, Beall, Loomis, Blascovich, & Turk, 2005). A man could readily present himself as a woman and vice versa. A child could take on the role of a soldier. A criminal could be placed in the shoes of his or her victim. In short, avatars allow players to portray the self while simultaneously transforming the self.

Accordingly, different video games may call for different types of self-presentation. While playing a competitive first-person shooter video game, an individual may present him- or herself as menacing, tough, or intimidating. In a puzzle video game, a player might want to present him- or herself as more thoughtful and clever. Whether or not the game is multiplayer or single player likely impacts these choices as well.

In addition to the flexibility of self-presentation in video games, the nature of the self-presentation can impact user attitudes and behaviors. According to self-perception theory (Bem, 1972; Poortinga, Whitmarsh, & Suffolk, 2013), individuals understand their own attitudes and beliefs as outsiders, assessing themselves through the circumstances in which they are acting. When given certain external cues, a person will likely adapt his or her behavior to accommodate that cue. For example, an individual cued with his or her avatar's race may have racial stereotypes activated. This activation might cause the user to act in accordance with the activated stereotypes. The stereotype that blacks are aggressive or that Asians are intelligent would cue a player to use a black or Asian avatar in a way that matches those stereotypes (Weber, Lavine, Huddy, & Federico, 2014). In that fashion, using an avatar can transform the understanding of the self to accommodate the identity of the avatar.

In one of the original, illustrative 1967 studies of this phenomenon, Bem claimed that the way in which people evaluated their attitudes and behaviors was no different than how an observer evaluated others' attitudes. This indicates that people are trained and conditioned to observe themselves as others might view them. When a child has butterflies in his or her stomach, he or she understands that feeling not because of the traits intrinsic to that feeling but because descriptions of the feeling have been learned as described by an outsider (Bem, 1972); thus a child's understanding of the feeling is derived from outside observations rather than intrinsic understanding. People learn a lot about someone's attitudes by observing behaviors and the same is true of observing the self. One example of this can be found in Valins' (1966) study. In this study men were shown images of a woman while hearing what they perceived to be their own heartbeats. However, the heartbeats were manipulated. When the experimenter made the heartbeat recording beat faster, the men interpreted the increase in heart rate as attraction to the woman in the photo. In conclusion, the men were making inferences about their feelings toward the woman based on their observations of themselves rather than how they actually felt.

For another example of self-perception theory, Frank and Gilovich (1988) hypothesized, based on stereotypes, that participants in black uniforms would perceive themselves as more aggressive than those wearing other colored uniforms. Results confirmed these predictions. Self-perception theory has interesting applications to mass media, particularly video games. A Peña,

Hancock, and Merola (2009) study effectively demonstrated the phenomenon in a video game environment. In this study, participants were assigned an avatar that appeared to be a member of the Ku Klux Klan (KKK) or a doctor. Participants demonstrated more thoughts and behaviors congruent with stereotypes of the avatar they were assigned such that those using a KKK avatar were more aggressive and those assigned a doctor avatar were more altruistic. Expanding on this, Yee, Bailenson, and Ducheneaut (2009) performed two studies demonstrating how avatars could influence behavior. Participants who used attractive and tall avatars demonstrated better task performance than those with unattractive and shorter avatars. Likewise, participants using tall avatars were more assertive in a money splitting task than those with shorter avatars. This study draws on the notion that tall, attractive people are often perceived as being more qualified for certain leadership tasks.

The Proteus effect stems from these studies of self-perception theory in order to accommodate the phenomenon in virtual settings. This effect describes how people may adapt personal behaviors to conform to the behaviors expected of their digital representations in a virtual environment, or avatars (Fox, Bailenson, & Tricase, 2013; Yee & Bailenson, 2007). The Proteus effect is particularly salient in video games because playing video games often simulates being a media character or someone in a specific social role (Klimmt, Hefner, & Vorderer, 2009). Video games are distinct from more passive forms of media in which the audience has a dyadic relationship with media characters, whereas in video games, the user and character are merged socially and psychologically (Klimmt et al., 2009). For example, a user may perceive him- or herself to be stronger or more courageous if he or she assumes the role of a soldier in a video game. Indeed, individuals who played video games displayed more likelihood to emulate the game content than individuals who only observed the game content (Fox et al., 2013; Peng, 2008). Again, this highlights the difference between playing a video game and consuming other types of more traditional media.

In summary, video games offer many opportunities for self-presentation that are not found in other forms of media. And self-presentation is a two-way street such that players can influence their presentation in video games but the presentation can also impact the player. Thus, self-presentation is an important consideration when thinking about the impact of video games.

REFERENCES

Ahn, S. J. (2011). Embodied experiences in immersive virtual environments: Effects on proenvironmental attitude and behavior. Unpublished doctoral dissertation. Stanford University, Stanford, CA.

Apperley, T. H. (2006). Genre and game studies: Toward a critical approach to video game genres. *Simulation & Gaming, 37*(1), 6–23.

Ariely, D. (2000). Controlling the information flow: Effects on consumers' decision making and preferences. *Journal of Consumer Research, 27*(2), 233–248.

Ashby, W. R. (1956). *An introduction to cybernetics.* Englewood Cliffs, NJ: Prentice Hall

Bailenson, J., Beall, A., Loomis, J., Blascovich, J., & Turk, M. (2004). Transformed social interaction: Decoupling representation from behavior and form in collaborative virtual environments. *Presence: Teleoperators & Virtual Environments, 13*(4), 428–441.

Bailenson, J., Beall, A., Loomis, J., Blascovich, J., & Turk, M. (2005). Transformed social interaction, augmented gaze, and social influence in immersive virtual environments. *Human Communication Research, 31*(4), 511–537.

Bailenson, J., & Yee, N. (2006). A longitudinal study of task performance, head movements, subjective report, simulator sickness, and transformed social interaction in collaborative virtual environments. *Presence: Teleoperators & Virtual Environments, 15*(6), 699–716.

Bandura, A. (2002). Social cognitive theory of mass communication. *Media Effects.* Mahwah, NJ: Lawrence Erlbaum Associates, Publishers.

Baumeister, R. F. (1998). The self. In D. T. Gilbert, S. T. Fiske, & G. Lindzey (Eds.), *Handbook of social psychology* (4th ed., pp. 680–740). New York: McGraw-Hill.

Beedie, C. J., Lane, A. M., & Wilson, M. (2012). A possible role for emotion and emotion regulation in physiological responses to false performance feedback in 10km laboratory cycling. *Applied Psychophysiology and Biofeedback, 37*(4), 269–277.

Bem, D. (1972). Self perception theory. In L. Berkowitz (ed.), *Advances in experimental social psychology* (Vol. 6, pp. 2–57). New York: Academic Press.

Bem, D. (1967). Self-perception: An alternative interpretation of cognitive dissonance phenomena. *Psychological Review, 74*(3), 183–200.

Bowlby, J. (1982). Attachment and loss: Retrospect and prospect. *American Journal of Orthopsychiatry, 54*(2), 664–678.

Bowman, R. F. (1982). A Pac-Man theory of motivation. Tactical implications for classroom instruction. *Educational Technology, 22*(9), 14–17.

Bucy, E. (2004). Interactivity in society: Locating an elusive concept. *Information Society, 20*(5), 373–383.

Buist, E. (2014). Should thieves in World of Warcraft be sent to real prisons? *TheGuardian.com.* http://www.theguardian.com/technology/shortcuts/2014/jul/24/thieves-world-warcraft-real-prisons-tory-mike-weatherley

Carpenter, J., Brockopp, D., & Andrykowski, M. (1999). Self-transformation as a factor in the self-esteem and well-being of breast cancer survivors. *Journal of Advanced Nursing, 29*(6), 1402–1411.

Carver, C., & Scheier, M. (2001). *On the self-regulation of behavior.* Cambridge, UK: Cambridge University Press.

Connellan, T., & Zemke, R. (1993). *Sustaining knock your socks off service.* New York: AMACOM Books.

Consalvo, M. (2005). Rule sets, cheating, and magic circles: Studying games and ethics. *International Review of Information Ethics, 4*(2), 7–12.

Consalvo, M. (2009). There is no magic circle. *Games and Culture. 4*(4)

Cooper, H. & Veloria, L. (2012). *Halo 4* vs. *Call of Duty: Black Ops 2. Gamesradar.com.* http://www.gamesradar.com/halo-4-vs-call-duty-black-ops-2/

Dibbell, J. (1993). A rape in cyberspace. *The Village Voice,* 36–42

Dietz, T. L. (1998). An examination of violence and gender role portrayals in videogames: Implications for gender socialization and aggressive behaviour. *Sex Roles, 38*(5/6), 425–442.

Engelkamp, J., & Zimmer, H. D. (2002). Free recall and organization as a function of varying relational encoding in action memory. *Psychological Research, 66*(2), 91.

ESRB.org (2014a). Education & outreach. *ESRB.org.* http://www.esrb.org/about/education.jsp

ESRB.org (2015). ESRB ratings guide. *ESRB.org.* http://www.esrb.org/ratings/ratings_guide. jsp

ESRB.org (2014b). FAQ. *ESRB.org.* http://www.esrb.org/ratings/faq.jsp#2

Fairfield, J. (2009). The magic circle. *Vanderbilt Journal of Entertainment and Technology Law, 11*(4): 823.

Fox, J., Bailenson, J. N., & Tricase, L. (2013). The embodiment of sexualized virtual selves: The Proteus effect and experiences of self-objectification via avatars. *Computers in Human Behavior, 29*(3), 930–938.

Frank, M., & Gilovich, T. (1988). The dark side of self and social perception: Black uniforms and aggression in professional sports. *Journal of Personality and Social Psychology, 54,* 74–85.

Frasca, G. (2003). Simulation versus narrative. *The Video Game Theory Reader,* 221–235.

Gallaga, O. (2012). Keynote speaker Baratunde Thurston knows SXSW Interactive well. *Thestatesman.com* http://www.statesman.com/life/keynote-speaker-baratunde-thurston-knows-sxsw-interactive-well-2214254.html

Glanz, K., Schoenfeld, E. R., & Steffen, A. (2010). A randomized trial of tailored skin cancer prevention messages for adults: Project SCAPE skin cancer awareness, prevention and education. *American Journal of Public Health, 100*(4), 735–741.

Goetz, T. (2011). Harnessing the power of feedback loops. *Wired.* http://www.wired.com/magazine/2011/06/ff_feedbackloop/

Grodal, T. (2000). Video games and the pleasures of controls. In Zillmann, D. & Vorderer, P. (Eds.), *Media entertainment: The psychology of its appeal* (186–201). Mahwah, NJ: Lawrence Erlbaum Associates, Publishers.

Gu, J., Zhong, C., & Page-Gould, E. (2013). Listen to Your Heart: When False Somatic Feedback Shapes Moral Behavior. *Journal of Experimental Psychology: General, 142*(2), 307–312.

Hattie, J., & Timperley, H. (2007). The power of feedback. *Review of Educational Research, 77*(1), 81–112.

Haug, S., Meyer, C., Ulbricht, S., Gross, B., Rumpf, H., & John, U. (2010). Need for cognition as a predictor and a moderator of outcome in a tailored letters smoking cessation intervention. *Health Psychology, 29*(4), 367–373.

Hawkins, R. P., Kreuter, M., Resnicow, K., Fishbein, M., & Dijkstra, A. (2008). Understanding tailoring in communicating about health. *Health Education Research, 23*(3), 454–466.

Haynes, J. (2008). Dead Space review. *Ign.com.* http://www.ign.com/articles/2008/10/23/dead-space-review?page=3

Huizinga, J. (2014). *Homo Ludens Ils 86.* Oxon, UK: Routledge.

Ivory, J. D., Williams, D., Martins, N., & Consalvo, M. (2009). Good clean fun? A content analysis of profanity in videogames and its prevalence across game systems and ratings. *CyberPsychology & Behaviour, 12,* 1–4.

Jenkins, H. (2006). Reality bytes: Eight myths about video games debunked. *Impact of Gaming Essays.* http://www.pbs.org/kcts/videogamerevolution/impact/myths.html

Jensen, J. F. (1998). Interactivity: Tracking a new concept in media and communication studies. *Nordicom Review, 19,* 185–204.

Juul, J. (2010). *A casual revolution: Reinventing video games and their players.* Cambridge, MA: MIT Press.

Juul, J. (2011). *Half-real: Video games between real rules and fictional worlds.* Cambridge, MA: MIT Press.

Kalyanaraman, S., & Sundar, S. S. (2008). Impression formation effects in online mediated communication. In E. Konijn, S. Utz, M. Tanis, & S. Barnes (Eds.), *Mediated interpersonal communication* (217–233). New York: Routledge.

Katz, J. (2008). Virtual 'Maple Story' murder reveals online lives gone too far. *Findingdulcinea.com.* http://www.findingdulcinea.com/news/technology/September-October-08/Virtual--Maple-Story--Murder-Reveals-Online-Lives-Gone-Too-Far.html

Klimmt, C., Hefner, D., & Vorderer, P. (2009). The video game experience as "true" identification: A theory of enjoyable alterations of players' self-perception. *Communication Theory (10503293), 19*(4), 351–373.

Kluger, A. N., & DeNisi, A. (1996). The effects of feedback interventions on performance: A historical review, a meta-analysis and a preliminary feedback intervention theory. *Psychological Bulletin, 119,* 254–284.

Lancaster, B., & Palframan, J. (2009). Coping with major life events: the role of spirituality and self-transformation. *Mental Health, Religion & Culture, 12*(3), 257–276.

Lee J., Luchini, K., Michael, B., Norris, C., & Soloway, E. (2004). More than just fun and games: Assessing the value of educational video games in the classroom. Paper presented at the Conference on Human Factors in Computing Systems.

LeFebve, R. (2012). Interactive adventure game wows Exploratorium crowds. *Venturebeat.com.* http://venturebeat.com/2012/03/02/interactive-adventure-game-wows-exploratorium-crowds/

Legarie, D. (2012). *Halo 4* vs. *Call of Duty: Black Ops 2* . *Ign.com* . https://www.youtube.com/watch?v=UFaUh0Kkn5Q

Lessig, L. (2006). *Code.* New York: Lawrence Lessig.

Leung, S., Virwaney, S., Lin, F., Armstrong, A. J., & Dubbelboer, A. (2013). TSI-enhanced pedagogical agents to engage learners in virtual worlds. *International Journal of Distance Education Technologies, 11*(1), 1–13.

Lim, J., Zhan, A., Ko, J., Terzis, A., Szanton, S., & Gitlin, L. (2012). A closed-loop approach for improving the wellness of low-income elders at home using game consoles. *IEEE Communications Magazine, 50*(1), 44–51.

Loomis, J. M., Blascovich, J. J., & Beall, A. C. (1999). Immersive virtual environments as a basic research tool in psychology. *Behavior Research Methods, Instruments, and Computers, 31*(4), 557–564.

Martins, N., Williams, D., & Harrison, K. (2008). A content analysis of female body imagery in videogames. *Sex Roles.*

McGonigal, J. (2011). *Reality is broken: Why games make us better and how they can change the world.* New York: Penguin.

Miller, G. A., Galanter, E., & Pribram, K. H. (1960). *Plans and the Structure of Behavior.* New York: Henry Holt and Co.

Mindell, D. (2003). *Between human and machine: Feedback, control, and computing before cybernetics.* Baltimore, MD: Johns Hopkins University Press.

Montola, M. (2005). Exploring the edge of the magic circle: Defining pervasive games. In *Proceedings of DAC* (Vol. 1966, p. 103).

Muskus, J. (2008). New Wii games find a big (but stingy) audience. *New York Times.* http://www.nytimes.com/2008/04/21/technology/21wii.html?_r=1&ref=business

Noer, M. (2008). The future of video games. *Forbes.com.* http://www.forbes.com/2008/02/08/future-video-games-tech-future07-cx_mn_de_0211game.html

Old, S. R., & Naveh-Benjamin, M. (2008). Memory for people and their actions: Further evidence for an age-related associative deficit. *Psychology and Aging, 23*(2), 467–472.

Parlett, D. S. (1999). *The Oxford history of board games.* New York: Oxford University Press.

Peña, J., Hancock, J. T., & Merola, N. A. (2010). The priming effects of avatars in virtual settings. *Communication Research, 36*(6), 838–856.

Peng, W. (2008). The mediational role of identification in the relationship between experience mode and self-efficacy: Enactive role-playing versus passive observation. *CyberPsychology & Behavior, 11*, 649–652

Poortinga, W., Whitmarsh, L., & Suffolk, C. (2013). The introduction of a single-use carrier bag charge in Wales: Attitude change and behavioural spillover effects. *Journal of Environmental Psychology, 36*, 240–247.

Ramaprasad, A. (1983). On the definition of feedback. *Behavioral Science, 28*(1).

Reed, J. (2008). Xbox 360 to get UK price cut. *BBC.* http://news.bbc.co.uk/newsbeat/hi/newsbeat/newsid_7618000/7618515.stm

Reeves, J. (2012). Updated: 3 killed in powerful storms. *Pottsmerc.com.* http://www.pottsmerc.com/article/20120302/NEWS04/120309912/-1/traffic/powerful-storms-cause-damage-across-several-states

Reeves, B., & Read, J. L. (2013). *Total engagement: How games and virtual worlds are changing the way people work and businesses compete.* Boston: Harvard Business Press.

Reinecke, L., Tamborini, R., Grizzard, M., Lewis, R., Eden, A., & Bowman, N. (2012). Characterizing mood management as need satisfaction: The effects of intrinsic needs on selective exposure and mood repair. *Journal of Communication, 62*(3), 437–453.

Rogers, R. (2013). Concerning interactivity: Effective video game content analysis. Presented at the annual conference of the International Communication Association, London, UK.

Ruiter, R., Werrij, M. Q., & de Vries, H. (2010). Investigating message-framing effects in the context of a tailored intervention promoting physical activity. *Health Education Research*, *25*(2), 343–354.

Salen, K., & Zimmerman, E. (2004). *Rules of Play: Game Design Fundamentals*. Cambridge, MA: MIT Press.

Sherry, J. L. (2001). The effects of violent videogames on aggression: A meta-analysis. *Human Communication Research*, *27*(3), 409–431.

Senge, P.M. (1990). *The fifth discipline*. New York, NY: Doubleday.

Sundar, S., Kalyanaraman, S., & Brown, J. (2003). Explicating web site interactively: Impression formation effects in political campaign sites. *Communication Research*, *30*(1), 30–59.

Sundar, S., & Kim, J. (2005). Interactivity and persuasion: Influencing attitudes with information and involvement. Paper presented at the annual conference of the International Communication Association, 1.

Telegraph.co.uk. (2012). Online game theft earns real-world conviction. *Telegraph.co.uk*. http://www.telegraph.co.uk/technology/video-games/9053870/Online-game-theft-earns-real-world-conviction.html

Teo, H. H., Oh, L. B., Liu, C., & Wei, K. K. (2003). An empirical study of the effects of interactivity on Web user attitude. *International Journal of Human Computer Studies*, *58*, 281–305.

Thiemann, K. S., & Goldstein, H. (2001). Social stories, written text cues, and video feedback: Effects on social communication of children with autism. *Journal of Applied Behavior Analysis*, *34*(4), 425–446.

Thompson, K. M., & Haninger, K. (2001). Violence in E-rated videogames. *JAMA*, *286*, 591–598.

Thompson, K. M., Tepichin, K., & Haninger, K. (2006). Content and ratings of mature-rated videogames. *Archives of Pediatrics & Adolescent Medicine 160*(4): 402–410.

Valins, S. (1966). Cognitive effects of false heart-rate feedback. *Journal of Personality and Social Psychology*, *4*, 400–408.

Warren, M. (1992). Democratic theory and self-transformation. *The American Political Science Review*, *86*(1), 8.

Weber, C. R., Lavine, H., Huddy, L., & Federico, C. M. (2014). Placing racial stereotypes in context: social desirability and the politics of racial hostility. *American Journal of Political Science*, *58*(1), 63–78.

Wiener, N. (1961). *Cybernetics: Or, control and communication in the animal and the machine*. Cambridge, MA: MIT Press.

Winne, P. H., & Butler, D. L. (1994). Student cognition in learning from teaching. In T. Husen & T. Postlethwaite (Eds.), *International encyclopedia of education* (2nd ed., pp. 5738–5745). Oxford: Pergamon.

Wood, R. T. A., Griffiths, M. D., Chappell, D., & Davies, M. N. O. (2004). The structural characteristics of video games: A psycho-structural analysis. *Cyberpsychology & Behavior*, *7*(1), 1–10.

Yee, N., & Bailenson, J. (2007). The Proteus effect: The effect of transformed self-representation on behavior. *Human Communication Research*, *33*(3), 271–290.

Yee, N., Bailenson, J. N., & Ducheneaut, N. (2009). The Proteus effect: Implications of transformed digital self-representation on online and offline behavior. *Communication Research*, *36*, 285–312.

II

The Positive

Chapter Two

Education

In interviews with video games players, one player known as Lucifer641 in the online gaming community said that playing video games taught him more about War War II, specifically the Battle of Stalingrad, than any history course he had ever taken in his formal education (Rogers, 2012). He was referring to one of the stages in the video game series *Call of Duty* that takes place during World War II. In one mission the player assumes the role of a Russian sniper during the Battle of Stalingrad. This sentiment is not unique and there is much evidence that video games are valuable teaching tools. Indeed, video games have been used as effective educational tools. Video games have been connected to improved problem solving skills (Lopez & Caceres, 2010), improved probabilistic inference (Green, Pouget, & Bavelier, 2010), and improved spatial rotation tasks (Spence & Feng, 2010). Simulations or games have helped orthopedic surgeons and other medical professionals develop their skills (Cowan et al., 2010; Graafland, Schraagen, & Schijven, 2012) and video games are also tied to improvements in students' typing, reading, politics, financial skills, resource management, and engineering (Prensky, 2005).

It is worth noting that a distinction has been made between serious games and non-serious games. Serious games are video games meant for purposes other than pure entertainment such as education and behavior change while non-serious games are meant for entertainment/commercial purposes (Connolly, Boyle, MacArthur, Hainey, & Boyle, 2012). Some examples of serious games are *Darfur is Dying*, a game that simulates being in a refugee camp, and *IBM CityOne*, a city-building game that describes how complex systems interact with one another within a city's infrastructure. In both cases, the games are used to educate players and raise awareness on a topic, not to just entertain. Goals of serious games might include political activism or advertising as well as education. Meanwhile, non-serious games, such as *Call of Duty* and *Halo*, are more well-known and meant for primarily entertainment and commercial purposes. Notably, education can be a by-product of non-serious games as well. As such, this chapter examines both serious and non-serious games. To date, a handful of frameworks have been put forth regarding how video games impact learning.

In one of James Paul Gee's (2003) seminal works, he asserts that video games are "learning machines." In other words, they train users in certain lessons and encourage users to learn the way the game works. In fact, a game's success depends on its ability to educate its players effectively. Players find video games frustrating and not worth the effort when the games do not provide adequate instruction. As such, Gee asserts that many "good" video games have already solved one of the major problems facing educators worldwide: *How to get people to enjoy learning difficult lessons.* Gee (2005) uses the video game *System Shock 2* to explain how video games work to educate players. In this game information kiosks are placed in key areas such that the player will learn information from them and then apply the information to the game. Players learn by doing in *System Shock 2* (Shaffer, Halverson, Squire, & Gee, 2005). This is common in many games. As a result, the player learns how to play but also gets to *feel* the play and gauge it on his or her own terms.

Prenksy (2005) details five levels of game based learning:

1. Video games teach players *how to do something*. Early in video games, players need to learn how the game functions. Prensky indicates that this shows how repetition is valuable for learning outcomes.
2. Second, players learn *what to do and what not to do*. Players learn the rules and parameters of the game. Many games integrate tutorials directly into game play so the rules are clear. For example, in a flight game, *Strike Suit Zero*, the first mission in the game teaches the rules of the game while playing. This teaches rules in practice, not in the abstract. Players can see how the rules worked as they learn them. According to Prensky (2005), doing so encourages players to evaluate rules and determine which are fair or valuable and which are unfair or detrimental.
3. Games also teach *why things happen*. Prensky (2005) argues that players learn strategies within the context of why things happen. In other words, players figure out how to function within a game effectively, what works and what does not.
4. Players learn about *context of various situations*. Games immerse players in a culture where they must learn what has value and what does not in order to succeed. Players learn the "where" of the game.

5. Players can *do things in the game space that they cannot do in the physical world*. Video games present situations in which certain behaviors are appropriate. These behaviors may not be appropriate in the physical world. See the previous discussion of the magic circle for examples. Prensky argues that this requires players to evaluate the consistencies and inconsistencies of their actions in the game and in the physical world. Both the classroom and a video game can be considered magic circles or isolated spots where special rules pertain (Huizinga, 2014). The rules of the classroom/video games simultaneously can simulate the rules of the "real" world but students/players are insulated from rules in the "real" world, allowing for safe and comfortable learning environments. This allows students and players to make mistakes without suffering "real" consequences.

Fundamental to this framework is that video games can get people to enjoy learning difficult lessons because they are entertaining, motivating, gratifying, emotional, and involving (Prensky, 2005).

Similarly, the General Learning Model (GLM) uses cognitive theories to explain this phenomenon (Buckley & Anderson, 2006). The GLM is based on the General Aggression Model, which is discussed in detail in this book's violence chapter. In short, the GLM indicates that students learn through repetition provided in games and games provide a simulated environment that can enhance students' ability for trial and error in unique scenarios. From there, games can alter automatically accessed knowledge structures to help students learn more effectively.

Meanwhile, Annetta (2010) outlines a handful of critical components for educational games:

- Identity or self-presentation in a virtual world increases investment in the virtual world. If the virtual world encourages learning then learning goals should be salient to the player represented in the game.
- Immersion helps gamers to become motivated to accomplish in-game goals. When players feel immersed, they are more likely to achieve a flow state. A flow state is when skill is appropriately matched with challenge and an individual becomes absorbed in what he or she is doing (Csikszentmihalyi, 2014). If skill outweighs challenge then the game will be boring. If challenge outweighs skill then the game will be frustrating.
- Annetta also describes a feedback system in terms of interactivity such that input and output messages are related. These feedback systems in games can help build specific skills for students.
- Educational games should also increase in complexity so that they challenge multiple skill levels and build upon previous knowledge. This parallels effective game design.

- Lastly, informed teaching and instruction should also be included so that student progress can be effectively evaluated and managed.

Another framework describes rich environments for active learning (REALs), Grabinger and Dunlap (1995). REALS offer a series of learning assumptions relevant to education:

- Complex situations facilitate transfer of knowledge from the classroom.
- Learners should be allowed to create meaning in their lessons not just receive information.
- Students learn more when they are collaborating with one another than when they are not.
- Students should be placed in situations in which they must use critical thinking and problem solving skills
- Learners can assess their own needs and experiences when learning.
- Skills are most effectively learned in realistic contexts.

REALs incorporate each of these attributes and, in turn, develop student responsibility, initiative, and decision-making (Grabinger & Dunlap, 1995). Based on these assumptions, a video game can be a REAL. Consider a flight simulator intended to train amateurs to fly an airplane. A flight simulator video game: presents a complex scenario (flying an airplane), immerses players in the realistic context where they must make decisions and assess their needs.

One final framework for understanding video games and education can be understood as epistemographic frames. Many games have their own epistemology, or how players know what they know. Some have suggested that games are particularly effective in educating because they can shift players' epistemographic frames (Nash & Shaffer, 2013). This means that players start to think in a certain way when playing a game. In other words, games place players in situations where they are asked to alter their frame of mind. This allows players to see which practices work and which do not. Moments of failure force players to reevaluate their thinking. The speed and efficiency of this learning presents key scenarios for learning and eliminates minutiae (Shaffer et al., 2005). In an educational context, learners can be placed directly into the most critical points for acquiring knowledge. For example, the video game *Game Dev Story* puts the player in the role of a video game developer. The object of the game is to create a successful business within the video game industry. Players are required to make staffing and work flow decisions. The feedback systems in place encourage a specific way of thinking and problem solving. Players are placed into the role of a video game developer and learn how to think and act like a game developer. That is, video games require players to think like their self-presentations. Shaffer and colleagues (2005) illustrate this with the video game *Full Spectrum Warrior*, a video game based on U.S. military training. As such, the game requires players to think and act like soldiers. Players are given new identities and informed on what it is like to be in a certain combat situation. Thus, players are trained to think in a certain way consistent with their self-presentation. It is worth noting that players can also be placed in abstract situations not easily replicated in the physical world (Shaffer et al., 2005). For example, the video game *Foldit* allows players to fold proteins.

All of these frameworks offer insight into how video games impact learning. In order to reconcile each, it seems logical to explain the benefits of video games in terms of the psychological advantages they engender. Using games for education is associated with higher student engagement (Annetta, Minogue, Holmes, & Cheng, 2009), enjoyment (Hicks & Higgins, 2010), greater use of attention (Greenfield, DeWinstanley, Kilpatrick & Kaye, 1994) as well as an increased sense of presence, involvement, and arousal (Ivory & Kalyanaraman, 2007). The idea, then, is that video games enhance psychological states conducive to learning. Indeed, playing commercial video games can impact brain plasticity (Kühn, Gleich, Lorenz, Lindenberger, & Gallinat, 2014).

While video games can be a valuable educational tool, they are not a panacea for education. There are many barriers to using video games in the classroom. For example, playing a game can increase cognitive load, making learning more cumbersome (deHaan, Reed, & Kuwada, 2010). Drawing upon and extrapolating from this literature, this book posits that the efficacy of video games in the classroom can be explained via rules, feedback, and self-presentation with special attention to psychological states. The remainder of the chapter will be dedicated to these topics.

Rules define a classroom's structure (Boostrom, 1991). In the same fashion, rules define the structure of video games (Juul, 2011). Rules in a classroom are implemented to achieve learning goals. In other words, rules are intended to lead to learning outcomes. For example, in a journalism class, the instructor may not accept late assignments. Many students may find this rule to be extremely harsh. However, in the journalism industry deadlines are extremely important. Stories need to be turned in on time for the printing press or produced in time to go on air. As a result, this "no late assignments" rule teaches the students about industry practices and trains them to become effective journalists. Video games operate the same way such that they teach the values of the game.

In most games, rules are introduced early to players and the rules are intended to help players understand deeper nuances later in the game. Rules are introduced and iterated upon as the game progresses. In doing so, a well-designed video game can inform best practices for pedagogy. Juul (2012) describes how rules should work in video games and applying these descriptions to classrooms is a meaningful exercise. In both games and classrooms, rules should: provide understandable guidelines, create challenge, help users learn how to improve/sharpen skills, emphasize different challenges, and distinguish a class/games from others. Juul also notes that rules should interact with the user and create a "machine" that responds to player action and helps users learn. Juul is describing the concept of feedback. Classrooms are effective when they implement a feedback loop, are interactive, and "active." Active learning, or learning in which the student is engaged in the learning process, is an effective teaching strategy and leads to improved learning outcomes and more consistent outcomes than passive learning (Freeman et al., 2014; Krogh & Vedelsby, 1995; Myers & Jones, 1993).

Feedback, at its most fundamental, is education or training. Feedback trains users to act in accordance with certain goals, in this case: educational goals. For example, grades in classrooms are a form of feedback that helps students pursuing learning goals (Hattie & Timperley, 2007) and many of the desired psychological outcomes for education are related to feedback (Glanz, Schoenfeld, & Steffen, 2010; Hattie & Timperley, 2007; Hawkins, Kreuter, Resnicow, Fishbein, & Dijkstra, 2008; Kluger & DeNisi, 1996).

In terms of self-presentation, when a player uses an avatar, or a graphic virtual character that represents someone or something in a computer environment (Holzwarth, Janiszewski, & Neumann, 2010), the player merges psychologically with the avatar (Klimmt, Hefner, & Vorderer, 2009; Lewis et al., 2009; Yee & Bailenson, 2007). When the player *becomes* the character, he or she adopts attitudes and behaviors consistent with the character (Klimmt, Hefner, Vorderer, Roth, & Blake, 2010). While this phenomenon has been well documented, the use of avatars in an educational context is underexplored. Included below is a study that posits assigning an avatar with specific attributes related to learning goals can advance pedagogical outcomes (Rogers, 2014). Specifically, this study argues that avatars are valuable educational tools such that assigning students with avatars whose goals match the goals of the educational task will improve performance on the task. For example, assigning a student an avatar that is a mathematician will encourage the student to act in accordance with what is expected of a mathematician. Consequently, this student's performance on math-related tasks should improve.

Importantly, when a task is perceived to be difficult it is more taxing and requires more cognitive resources. Cognitive resources are limited and, when depleted, tasks become cumbersome (Shiv & Fedorikhin, 1999). "Cognitive overload"—the prevailing state when a user's capacity for mental processes is depleted—is a challenge for learning goals (Mayer & Moreno, 2003). Essentially, when an individual perceives that a task is difficult, cognitive resources will be more depleted than if the task is simple, making a student less capable of successfully completing a task (Drolet & Luce, 2004; Hattie

& Timperley, 2007; Ward & Mann, 2000). Furthermore, perceptions of difficulty impact self-esteem (Hattie & Timperley, 2007; Pajares & Schunk, 2001) and persistence on tasks (Baumeister, 1998; Di Paula & Campbell, 2002; Schunk, 1995). Both of which can impact performance on tasks (Akgunduz, 2015; Hattie & Timperley, 2007; Schunk, 1991; Schunk, 1995). Ultimately, avatars that are meant to excel at certain tasks will encourage their users to feel that they can excel at the task as well. In other words, if the avatar should think a task is easy, then its user will think the task is easy as well. When an avatar should think a task is difficult or has no connection to the task, the task will seem more difficult. Due to alterations in perceived difficulty, performance will improve.

In this study, participants were randomly assigned to one of two conditions in which they were given an avatar that appeared in their browser window. One avatar was a student and one was an average person. Then, the participants performed a series of tasks in the browser window. These tasks tested reading comprehension and math skills (tasks related to performance in school). Participants were then asked to rank how difficult the tasks were.

The main outcome was task performance. This was measured in two ways. First it was measured through *reading comprehension score*. Participants were asked to read a short, 25-line passage then answer a series of questions related to the passage. Second, task performance was assessed through *math score*. Participants were asked to solve a series of elementary math equations. Both the reading comprehension questions and the math questions were based on high school standardized tests sample questions. The potential mechanism explored was *perceived difficulty*.

Analysis revealed no significant effects of avatar type on task performance. Thus, avatar type had no impact on reading comprehension score and math score. However, there was a significant effect of avatar type on perceived difficulty such that participants assigned a generic avatar perceived the tasks to be significantly more difficult than those assigned a student avatar. Further analysis revealed that lower feelings of difficulty led to higher scores on reading comprehension and math. In summary, avatar type did not impact task performance directly. However, participants assigned a student avatar perceived the task to be less difficult and that led to improved performance on both reading comprehension score and math score.

Based on previous research, the student avatar should have positively impacted performance. Importantly, the outcomes tested in previous studies were limited to psychological or cognitive characteristics, not performance on potentially challenging tasks. These findings suggest that avatars may be less effective in provoking behaviors when the behavior requires knowledge or skills. It seems plausible that some participants, regardless of their avatar, would have less ability to answer these questions than others; a limitation of the effects of avatars. As such, there should be a distinction between psychological measures and task performance measures when it comes to avatar influence.

Accordingly, avatar type did impact psychological dimensions related to the task. The finding that those who were assigned a student avatar perceived the reading comprehension and math tasks to be easier than those assigned a generic avatar supports the notion that the avatar psychologically merged with the user. Those assigned an avatar that was a good student adopted the traits of a good student. In turn, the participants, when faced with a challenging educational task, felt that the task was easier than those who did not have a student avatar. Within the domain of education, this is a compelling finding. If students struggle with certain lessons, assigning them avatars might help ease that difficulty.

Importantly, there are instances when avatar assignment might actually impede task performance in a classroom. Based on the preceding literature and findings, it might seem like a good idea to provide an avatar to students that is an expert in a specific field to enhance task performance. However, this might actually work against desired outcomes. Assigning an avatar that has already made considerable progress on relevant tasks may actually hinder task performance. Feedback on progress is important to improving performance (Connellan & Zemke, 1993; Fleming & Levie, 2005; Gee, 2005). This is especially applicable to educational pursuits (Schunk & Swartz, 1993). Consumer behavior literature indicates that if a user perceives a large degree of progress toward a goal then the user will feel that the goal is attainable (Huang & Zhang, 2011) and perceptions of high progress suggest imminent goal completion, which gives users license to deviate from goal pursuit (Fishbach & Dhar, 2005). In other words, when users feel comfortable with their progress on a task, they do not maintain actions consistent with completing those tasks.

The supposition then is that assigning an avatar that is highly accomplished on related tasks will result in high perceptions of progress on those tasks and these high perceptions of progress will lead to a drop in task performance. An additional study explored this phenomenon (Rogers 2014). The procedure for this study replicated the previous study with a few exceptions. First, the student avatar was replaced with a reporter avatar. The reporter avatar was dressed professionally and was standing in front of a camera. The avatar was accompanied by text that read, "He/She is a news reporter with excellent journalism skills." Second, the reading comprehension and math tasks were replaced by tasks that were relevant to a reporter. Specifically, participants were asked to identify dimensions of newsworthiness as well as correct Associated Press style, which they were briefly trained on at the front end of the study. These items were based on undergraduate level journalism course goals. Instead of perceived difficulty, participants were asked about their *perceived progress* on the tasks.

Again, avatar type had no impact on task performance but avatar type did have an impact on perceived progress. Participants with a generic avatar perceived less progress than those assigned a reporter avatar. However, there were no indirect effects of avatar type on task performance. The lack of findings reinforces that avatar type does not impact task performance but those assigned a reporter avatar did not demonstrate higher scores on tasks related to associated press style or newsworthiness. Again, this shows that assigning an avatar does not imbue the user with skills that the avatar possesses. Instead, the avatar likely alters psychological dimensions related to that task.

On this point, the prediction that those with a reporter avatar, or an avatar that had already demonstrated success on the tasks, would perceive more progress on the tasks than those assigned a generic avatar, was supported. In this instance, the avatar, by already having professional accomplishments, conferred higher perceptions of progress than those using an avatar without professional accomplishments; although, avatar type had no impact on task performance via progress.

These two studies demonstrate that the impact of an avatar on pedagogical goals can depend on the type of avatar used. Namely, avatars that reduce perceived difficulty are ideal. In particular, this shows practical tactics for improving performance on educational tasks and also shows some critical conceptual differences when assigning avatars. Meanwhile, this highlights the importance of avoiding assigning avatars that might encourage negative traits in students such as aggression, apathy, or insubordination.

In conclusion, video games offer promising applications in education. However, their application is limited because video games can be difficult and expensive to produce. Further, many instructors do not include them in lessons as their applications are not always apparent (Torrente et al., 2009). The biggest problem facing educational games is that the ones that exist are not being implemented. However, thinking about educational games in terms of feedback, rules, and self-presentation offers solutions for improving the efficacy of video games, or game elements, in education.

REFERENCES

Akgunduz, Y. (2015). The influence of self-esteem and role stress on job performance in hotel businesses. *International Journal of Contemporary Hospitality Management, 27*(6), 1082–1099.

Annetta, L. A. (2010). The "I's" have it: A framework for serious educational game design. *Review of General Psychology, 14*(2), 105–112.

Annetta, L. A., Minogue, J., Holmes, S. Y., & Cheng, M. (2009). Investigating the impact of video games on high school students' engagement and learning about genetics. *Computers & Education , 53*(1), 74–85.

Baumeister, R. F. (1998). The self. In D. T. Gilbert, S. T. Fiske, & G. Lindzey (Eds.), *Handbook of social psychology* (4th ed., pp. 680–740). New York: McGraw-Hill.

Boostrom, R. (1991). The nature and functions of classroom rules. *Curriculum Inquiry*, 193–216.

Buckley, K. E., & Anderson, C. A. (2006). A theoretical model of the effects and consequences of playing video games. *Playing video games: Motives, responses, and consequences*, 363–378.

Connellan, T., & Zemke, R. (1993). *Sustaining knock your socks off service*. New York: AMACOM Books.

Connolly, T. M., Boyle, E. A., MacArthur, E., Hainey, T., & Boyle, J. M. (2012). A systematic literature review of empirical evidence on computer games and serious games. *Computers & Education, 59*(2), 661–686.

Cowan, B., Sabri, H., Kapralos, B., Porte, M., Backstein, D., Cristancho, S., & Dubrowski, A. (2010). A serious game for total knee arthroplasty procedure, education and training. *Journal of CyberTherapy and Rehabilitation, 3*(3), 285–298.

Csikszentmihalyi, M. (2014). *Flow* (pp. 227–238). Springer Netherlands.

deHaan, J., Reed, W. M., & Kuwada, K. (2010). The effect of interactivity with a music video game on second language vocabulary recall. *Language Learning & Technology, 14*(2), 74–94.

Di Paula, A., & Campbell, J. D. (2002). Self-esteem and persistence in the face of failure. *Journal of Personality and Social Psychology, 83*, 711–724.

Drolet, A., & Luce, M. (2004). The rationalizing effects of cognitive load on emotion-based trade-off avoidance. *Journal of Consumer Research, 31*(1), 63–77.

Fishbach, A., & Dhar, R. (2005). Goals as excuses or guides: The liberating effect of perceived goal progress on choice. *Journal of Consumer Research, 32*(3), 370–377.

Fleming, M., & Levie, W. H. (1993). *Instructional message design: Principles from the behavioral and cognitive sciences*. Englewood Cliffs, NJ: Educational Technology Publications.

Freeman, S., Eddy, S. L., McDonough, M., Smith, M. K., Okoroafor, N., Jordt, H., & Wenderoth, M. P. (2014). Active learning increases student performance in science, engineering, and mathematics. *Proceedings of the National Academy of Sciences, 111*(23), 8410–8415.

Gee, J. P. (2003). What video games have to teach us about learning and literacy. New York: Palgrave Macmillan

Gee, J. P. (2005). Learning by design: Good video games as learning machines. *ELearning, 2*(1), 5–16.

Glanz, K., Schoenfeld, E. R., & Steffen, A. (2010). A randomized trial of tailored skin cancer prevention messages for adults: Project SCAPE skin cancer awareness, prevention and education. *American Journal of Public Health, 100*(4), 735–741.

Graafland, M., Schraagen, J. M., & Schijven, M. P. (2012). Systematic review of serious games for medical education and surgical skills training. *British Journal of Surgery, 99*(10), 1322–1330.

Grabinger, R. S., & Dunlap, J. C. (1995). Rich environments for active learning: A definition. *Research in Learning Technology, 3*(2).

Green, C. S., Pouget, A., & Bavelier, D. (2010). Improved probabilistic inference as a general learning mechanism with action video games. *Current Biology, 20*(17), 1573–1579.

Greenfield, P. M., DeWinstanley, P., Kilpatrick, H., & Kaye, D. (1994). Action video games and informal education: Effects on strategies for dividing visual attention. *Journal of Applied Developmental Psychology, 15*(1), 105–123.

Grodal, T. (2000). Video games and the pleasures of controls. In Zillmann, D. & Vorderer, P. (Eds.), *Media entertainment: The psychology of its appeal* (186–201). Mahwah, NJ: Lawrence Erlbaum Associates, Publishers.

Hattie, J., & Timperley, H. (2007). The power of feedback. *Review of Educational Research, 77*(1), 81–112.

Hawkins, R. P., Kreuter, M., Resnicow, K., Fishbein, M., & Dijkstra, A. (2008). Understanding tailoring in communicating about health. *Health Education Research, 23*(3), 454-466.

Hicks, L., & Higgins, J. (2010). Exergaming: Syncing physical activity and learning. *Strategies: A Journal for Physical and Sport Educators, 24*(1), 18–21.

Holzwarth, M., Janiszewski, C., & Neumann, M. M. (2006). The influence of avatars on online consumer shopping behavior. *Journal of Marketing, 70*(4), 19–36. doi:10.1509/jmkg.70.4.19

Huang, S., & Zhang, Y. (2011). Motivational consequences of perceived velocity in consumer goal pursuit. *Journal of Marketing Research, 48*(6), 1045–1056.

Huizinga, J. (2014). *Homo Ludens Ils 86*. Oxon, UK: Routledge.

Ivory, J. D., & Kalyanaraman, S. (2007). The effects of technological advancement and violent content in video games on players' feelings of presence, involvement, physiological arousal, and aggression. *Journal of Communication, 57*(3), 532–555.

Juul, J. (2012). *A casual revolution: Reinventing video games and their players*. Cambridge, MA: MIT Press.

Klimmt, C., Hefner, D., & Vorderer, P. (2009). The Video Game Experience as "True" Identification: A Theory of Enjoyable Alterations of Players' Self-Perception. *Communication Theory, 19*(4), 351–373.

Klimmt, C., Hefner, D., Vorderer, P., Roth, C., & Blake, C. (2010). Identification with video game characters as automatic shift of self-perceptions. *Media Psychology, 13*(4), 323–338.

Kluger, A. N., & DeNisi, A. (1996). The effects of feedback interventions on performance: A historical review, a meta-analysis and a preliminary feedback intervention theory. *Psychological Bulletin, 119*, 254–284.

Krogh, A., & Vedelsby, J. (1995). Neural network ensembles, cross validation, and active learning. *Advances in Neural Information Processing Systems*, 231–238.

Kühn, S., Gleich, T., Lorenz, R. C., Lindenberger, U., & Gallinat, J. (2014). Playing *Super Mario* induces structural brain plasticity: gray matter changes resulting from training with a commercial video game. *Molecular Psychiatry, 19*(2), 265–271.

Lewis, M. L., Weber, R., & Bowman, N. (2009). "They may be pixels, but they're MY pixels:" Developing a metric of character attachment in role-playing video games. *Cyberpsychology & Behavior, 11*(4), 515–518.

Lopez, J. M. C., & Caceres, M. J. M. (2010). Virtual games in social science education. *Computers & Education, 55*(3), 1336–1345.

Mayer, R. E., & Moreno, R. (2003). Nine ways to reduce cognitive load in multimedia learning. *Educational Psychologist, 38*(1), 43–52.

Meyers, C. & Jones, T. B. (1993). *Promoting Active Learning. Strategies for the College Classroom*. Jossey-Bass Inc., San Francisco, CA

Nash, P., & Shaffer, D. W. (2013). Epistemic trajectories: mentoring in a game design practicum. *Instructional Science, 41*(4), 745–771.

Pajares, F., & Schunk, D. (2001). The development of academic self-efficacy. *Development of achievement motivation. United States*.

Prensky, M. (2005). Computer games and learning: Digital game-based learning. *Handbook of Computer Game Studies, 18*, 97–122.

Rogers, R. (2012). The virtual locker room: Hate speech and online gaming. *Journal of New Media and Culture, 8*(1).

Rogers, R. (2014). Who are you in the classroom? Avatars for learning and education. Presented at the annual conference of the Association for Education in Journalism and Mass Communication, Montreal, Quebec.

Schunk, D. H. (1991). Self-efficacy and academic motivation. *Educational Psychologist, 26*(3/4), 207.

Schunk, D. H. (1995). Self-efficacy and education and instruction. In J. E. Maddux (Ed.), *Self efficacy, adaptation, and adjustment: Theory, research, and application* (pp. 281–303). New York: Plenum Press.

Schunk, D. H., & Swartz, C. W. (1993). Goals and progress feedback: Effects on self-efficacy and writing achievement. *Contemporary Educational Psychology, 18*(3), 337–354.

Shaffer, D. W., Halverson, R., Squire, K. R., & Gee, J. P. (2005). Video games and the future of learning. WCER Working Paper No. 2005-4. *Wisconsin Center for Education Research (NJ1)*.

Shiv, B., & Fedorikhin, A. (1999). Heart and mind in conflict: The interplay of affect and cognition in consumer decision making. *Journal of Consumer Research, 26*(3), 278–292.

Spence, I., & Feng, J. (2010). Video games and spatial cognition. *Review of General Psychology, 14*(2), 92–104.

Torrente, J., Moreno-Ger, P., Martínez-Ortiz, I., & Fernandez-Manjon, B. (2009). Integration and deployment of educational games in e-learning environments: The learning object model meets educational gaming. *Journal of Educational Technology & Society, 12*(4), 359–371.

Ward, A., & Mann, T. (2000). Don't mind if I do: Disinhibited eating under cognitive load. *Journal of Personality And Social Psychology, 78*(4), 753–763

Yee, N., & Bailenson, J. (2007). The Proteus effect: The effect of transformed self-representation on behavior. *Human Communication Research, 33*(3), 271–290.

Chapter Three

Prosocial Behaviors

Later, this book will detail arguments regarding violent video games causing aggression in players; violence is readily associated with video games but there is also plenty of evidence that video games can actually increase helping, or prosocial, behaviors. While a violent video game might influence violent behaviors, a prosocial video game might promote prosocial behaviors. Aggressive acts are those intended to harm another and prosocial behaviors are acts in which one person helps another attain a positive outcome (Eisenberg, Fabes, & Spinrad, 2006; Wiegman, Kuttschreuter, & Baarda, 1992). A prosocial behavior should be voluntary and the positive outcomes for the other must be intentional (Eisenberg et al., 2006). Penner, Dovidio, Piliavin, and Schroeder, (2005) describe three levels of prosocial behavior.

- The meso level describes an individual helping another in a specific situation.
- The micro level describes prosocial behaviors in terms of biology and evolution.
- The macro level describes prosocial behaviors at the group or organization level.

Video games, primarily, provide opportunities for prosocial behavior at the meso level, less frequently at the macro level, and occasionally at the micro level.

There are a handful of games on the market that emphasize prosocial behaviors. *Animal Crossing* requires players to help others in their community. *From Dust* asks the player to alter the environment to ensure a civilization's survival. However, even in these games players can engage in antisocial or violent behaviors. For example, in *From Dust*, the player can deliberately kill members of the tribe or sacrifice certain members.

Conversely, there is a large cross section of games that are ostensibly violent but feature a large degree of prosocial behaviors as well as violent behaviors (Irvine, 2008). At the time this was written, the current best-selling video games were *Grand Theft Auto V* and *Pokemon Omega Ruby/Alpha Sapphire*. The ESRB description of *Grand Theft Auto V* follows:

> Players assume the role of three criminals whose storylines intersect within the fictional city of Los Santos. Players can switch between each character to follow his storyline, completing missions which often include criminal activities (e.g., stealing cars, executing heists, assassinating targets). Players use pistols, machine guns, sniper rifles, and explosives to kill various enemies (e.g., rival gang members); players also have the ability to shoot non-adversary civilians, though this may negatively affect players' progress as a penalty system triggers a broad police search.

Meanwhile, *Pokemon Omega Ruby/Alpha Sapphire* is described as follows:

> Players pit their collection of small creatures (known as Pokémon) against other trainers to become Pokémon League Champion. Players interact with characters from a fantasy land and engage in turn-based battles: selecting attack moves (e.g., Thunder Shock, Fusion Flare, Poison Jab) from menu screens. These encounters are accompanied by smacking/zapping sounds, colorful light bursts, and depletion of health meters.

Based on these descriptions, both of these games can be considered fairly violent. However, they both have portions of narrative or play that would be considered prosocial under the definitions described above. Video games often present complex characters and different scenarios. As a result, violence and prosocial behaviors in video games are not mutually exclusive (Granic, Lobel, & Engels, 2014). For example, in *Grand Theft Auto V* the player can rescue one of the characters' sons, prevent a construction accident, or catch a thief as well as run over pedestrians, commit burglary, and murder. Likewise, *Pokemon Omega Ruby/Alpha Sapphire* emphasizes battle but it also requires the player to aid townsfolk and care for creatures. Video games can be both violent and prosocial and the content is not as black and white as it is often presented.

Within the context of video games, prosocial behavior can take several different shapes of helping: cooperation, leveling, walkthroughs, and crowdsourcing. Many games offer cooperative game modes where players work through game objectives together. *Far Cry 4* and *Halo: Master Chief Collection* are games that feature these modes. However, there are also some games that allow more one-sided prosocial behaviors. In *Dark Souls*, individuals can summon the help of other players. This help allows the summoning player to advance through difficult areas of the game while the helping player receives a relatively minor resource increase as a reward for helping. People in the *Dark Souls* community refer to this as "jolly cooperation" (Peskadoshi, 2011). Sometimes players even give resources to each other in order to benefit another player or a group (Sneakyø, 2013). In the game, *Game of War: Fire Age* players collect wood, stone, and other resources. Players will store these resources in a "bank" or give them to another player to aid others' progress. While this may seem inconsequential, it may have taken these players hours to acquire these resources and it helps others become competitive more readily. These are examples of cooperation between players in video games but there are other forms of prosocial behavior in video games as well. However, these actions may not be completely prosocial based on Eisenberg et al.'s (2006) definition of prosocial. Specifically, players may not be performing these actions voluntarily if the game requires them to progress. If we accept that game play in and of itself is voluntary then the intent of the behavior might not be consistent with Eisenberg et al.'s definition. A player might be helping another in order to achieve a game goal, not necessarily to benefit the other player. Notably, a recent study on prosocial behavior asked "How often do characters help each other in this game?" and "How often do you help others in this game?" (Prot et al., 2014, p. 3). This book takes the position that some actions in video games may not be purely prosocial due to game requirements and rewards, although, many behaviors do qualify as prosocial. As a result, this chapter will detail common instances of prosocial behavior with the caveat that some may not be strictly prosocial based on the game's parameters and the player's intentions. Based on this, it is important to keep feedback and rules in mind when examining these prosocial behaviors. Often, prosocial behaviors are rewarded. Thus, the rules of the game might encourage or discourage prosocial behaviors. Likewise, the feedback loop is directly impacted by these rewards. By injecting these rewards the adjustment of behavior is funneled toward prosocial behaviors unless the reward is deemed not worth the increased effort/difficulty.

Many video games like *World of Warcraft*, *Borderlands*, and *DOTA 2*, allow players to level up, meaning that a character within the game can progress, become stronger, and unlock new skills or abilities. For example, in the video game *Borderlands*, a character gains experience points for each objective he or she completes. These experience points can then be spent on new skills such as faster weapon reload times or increased weapon damage. Thus, it is generally desirable to be at a higher level. Sometimes a player with a high level character will aid a lower level character by increasing the weaker character's level more quickly. Since higher level characters are stronger, they can defeat enemies and complete objectives more easily than lower level characters and thus the lower level character attains levels and rewards more readily than they would without the high level character's help.

There are also many user-generated game guides and walkthroughs living online; websites like *IGN.com* have guides for many commercial video games. These are typically documents that are designed to help other players figure out how to beat certain games or certain portions of certain games. Importantly, other players typically create these guides for free not the game creators who sometimes sell their own official guides. For example, the website *Gamefaqs.com* hosts thousands of user-generated guides. A single author might write these guides or the guide might be a "wiki" in which many authors share their experiences and expertise in a specific game. This type of prosocial behavior could be understood as meso level or macro level depending on its production and use.

When these guides are generated as wikis, they can be understood as crowdsourcing. Crowdsourcing is an "online, distributed problem-solving and production model that leverages the collective intelligence of online communities to serve specific organizational goals" (Brabham, 2013, p. xix). Brabham (2013) details four key ingredients for crowdsourcing:

1. An entity that needs a task performed.
2. A group that is willing to perform the task.
3. An environment for that work to take place.
4. Mutual benefit for all involved.

This final point might suggest that crowdsourcing does not qualify as prosocial based on Eisenberg et al.'s (2006) definition as the player might be engaging in the behavior primarily for selfish benefit.

One video game developer, Peter Molyneaux, developed a video game based on the concept of crowdsourcing. Billed as a "social experiment" *Curiousity: What's Inside the Cube?* was a simple game in which players tried to get to the center of a cube, made up of billions of smaller "cubelets," by tapping each tiny cubelet. Tapping a cubelet destroyed it and revealed the layer underneath. According to the developers, the game contained 69 billion cubelets (Ivan, 2013). The game was released on November 6, 2012, and completed on May 26, 2013. Many users were playing this game simultaneously so the work of removing the layers took considerably less time than if only one person had been playing. What is perhaps most fascinating about this game: Only one person, the one who destroyed the last cubelet, was able to discover what was in the center of the cube. In other words, many people were working toward a goal/reward that they had no guarantee of ever experiencing.

Despite the stereotype that video games are isolating (Griffiths, Davies, & Chappell, 2003), there is evidence that video game play actually enhances socialization. Indeed, children who reported playing the Famicom (the early Japanese version of the Nintendo Entertainment System) were more socially adept than students who did not play the Famicom (Shimai, Masuda, & Kishimoto, 1990) and family members tend to interact more with one another when they have a video game console (Mitchell, 1985). Similar results have been found more recently (Bowman, Kowert, & Cohen, 2015). Also, having a video game console can encourage children to see each other outside of school and interact socially (Colwell, Grady, & Rhaiti, 1995; Irvine, 2008). Despite this, children who play video games are judged to be less prosocial by their classmates (Schie & Wiegman, 1997, see chapter 1). Perhaps video games are replacing traditional social interaction such that children might be socializing with friends in virtual spaces instead of physical spaces.

Importantly, these examples of prosocial behaviors primarily relate to multiplayer video game experiences where several human players are interacting in the game space. However, prosocial behaviors occur in single player experiences as well. These experiences are quite common. In the game *D4: Dark Dreams Don't Die*, players attempt to solve a murder mystery. Along the way, players have the opportunity to help non-player characters (NPCs) with various tasks. For example, a woman on an airplane was very nervous about the safety of the plane. The player can check on various items around the plane to help calm her down. In *Spelunky*, players can rescue a NPC that is stranded in a perilous situation. People can demonstrate helping behaviors for virtual and physical beings in video games.

Up to this point in the chapter, the varying uses of prosocial behaviors *within* video games have been demonstrated. Now, this chapter will shift to evidence that prosocial video games might actually impact prosocial behaviors *outside* of video games. Broadly speaking, prosocial actions outside of a game might be primed by media content such that prosocial stimulus can lead to more prosocial interpretations and behaviors in response to subsequent stimuli (Roskos-Ewoldsen, Roskos-Ewoldsen, & Dillman-Carpentier, 2002). That is, playing a prosocial video game makes prosocial thoughts top of mind to the player. Furthermore, prosocial actions can be learned through observation of media characters (Bandura, 2001) and players may model prosocial behaviors seen performed in a video game. Based on these theoretical premises, playing a prosocial video game *should* impact prosocial behaviors. There is some literature that supports this supposition. Playing nonviolent games is related to an increase in prosocial outcomes (Buckley & Anderson, 2006) and exposure to prosocial television programs has been shown to promote prosocial behaviors in children (Ostrov, Gentile, & Crick, 2006).

In another study, middle-school students listed their favorite video games as well as how often they played these games and how often these games required players to help or hurt others (Gentile et al., 2009). This revealed that students who played more prosocial games engaged in more prosocial behaviors such as cooperation, sharing, emotional awareness, and empathy. Conversely, violent video games had a negative relationship with prosocial behaviors. In a follow-up study, children were asked to note how often they played video games with specific prosocial behaviors: helping behaviors or affectionate behaviors. Results showed a connection between prosocial video game play and subsequent prosocial behaviors like helping a friend. Similarly, performing prosocial behaviors led to more prosocial video game play. Gentile and colleagues (2009) called this two-way relationship an "upward spiral." In other words, playing a prosocial video game enforced prosocial behaviors but simultaneously predisposition toward prosocial behaviors encouraged the play of prosocial video games (Slater, Henry, Swaim, & Anderson, 2003). Any description of a behavior spiral such as this can be understood as a feedback loop (Slater, 2003) and is helpful in understanding the role of prosocial video game content. In a third and final experimental study by Gentile and colleagues (2009), college students played a prosocial game, a violent game, or a neutral game. The prosocial games were *Super Mario Sunshine* (the player cleans up pollution on a tropical island) and *Chibi Robo* (players do household chores and help various members of a family). The violent games were *Ty 2* (players need to destroy objects and defeat bosses) or *Crash Twinsanity* (the player uses another character as a weapon and as a skateboard). The neutral games were *Pure Pinball* (a pinball simulator) or *Super Monkey Ball Deluxe* (the player navigates a ball through a puzzle). After playing the game, the player assigned puzzles to another participant. The puzzles varied in difficulty such that some were easier to complete and some were more difficult to complete. Notably, if the person who was assigned the puzzles could complete a large number of them, he or she was given a cash reward. Thus, the player could be helpful to the other person by selecting easier puzzles and avoiding harder puzzles. As expected, those who played a violent game chose to assign more difficult puzzles and those who played a prosocial game were more likely to assign easier puzzles. Those who played a prosocial game were more likely to act in ways that aligned with prosocial behavior than those who played a violent or neutral game. Again, playing a violent game had a negative relationship with helping behaviors (Gentile et al., 2009).

Greitemeyer and Osswald (2010) performed four experiments to further explore this phenomenon. In the first study, participants played the video game *Lemmings*, a game in which players guide creatures through a series of obstacles, *Lamers*, a parody of *Lemmings* in which players try to kill the creatures with guns and explosives, or *Tetris*, a game in which players try to form lines with various geometric shapes. After playing the game, the researcher "accidentally" spilled a cup of pencils on the ground. Participants who had played the prosocial game helped the researcher clean up the pencils while those who played the violent or neutral game did not help the researcher clean up the pencils. In a follow-up study, participants only played *Lemmings* or *Tetris*, eliminating the violent video game condition. After the experiment was ostensibly over, participants were asked to help a confederate with his or her master's thesis. Those who had played the prosocial video game were willing to help the student with the thesis and were willing to spend more time helping with the thesis despite a lack of compensation. In a third study, players again played *Tetris* or *City Crisis*, a game in which players rescue people in peril with a helicopter. During the experiment, a confederate posing as an ex-boyfriend entered the lab and began harassing the experimenter. The "ex-boyfriend" became mildly aggressive with the experimenter as the conflict went on. A majority of the prosocial video game players intervened to help while less than a quarter of those playing the neutral game intervened. In the last experiment, Greitemeyer and Osswald (2010) used the same exercise from experiment 1 where a cup of pencils was spilled and had players perform a thought listing task. Participants who played the prosocial video game reported more prosocial thoughts and more pencils picked up than those in the neutral condition. In this final study, the suggestion is that prosocial games lead to prosocial thoughts and these thoughts lead to an increase in prosocial behavior. Neuroscience results reflect a similar pattern (Liu, Teng, Lan, Zhang, & Yao, 2015).

While many of these studies focus on the promotion of prosocial behaviors via video games, video games can also make players *less* aggressive (Greitemeyer & Osswald, 2009). In their first experiment, Greitemeyer and Osswald asked participants to play a prosocial video game or a neutral video game. Then, participants were provided with a story that they were asked to complete. One story involved a near traffic accident, another involved an inconsiderate friend, and the third revolved around a frustrating restaurant experience. Participants who had played the prosocial video game finished the story in less aggressive ways than those who played the neutral video game. A similar experiment was conducted with a word completion task as the outcome (Greitemeyer & Osswald, 2009). In word completion tasks, a participant is asked to complete a word based on a stem of letters. When someone has more aggressive thoughts, they are expected to complete the stem with more aggressive words than those who are not having aggressive thoughts. For example, the word stem KI_ _ can be completed as KISS (non-aggressive) or KILL (aggressive). Those who played a prosocial video game reported fewer aggressive words on this task than those playing a neutral video game.

Another study examined how prosocial video games might lessen schadenfreude, or taking pleasure in the misfortune of others, and increase feelings of empathy (Greitemeyer, Osswald, & Brauer, 2010). Again, participants played a prosocial video game, *Lemmings*, or a neutral video game, *Tetris*. Then, they read a story about Paris Hilton in unfortunate circumstances and an essay by a student who was under duress. Those who played the prosocial game derived less pleasure from Paris Hilton's misfortune and showed more empathy toward the student in need.

These results, however, are not always uniform (Chambers & Ascione, 1987; Wiegman & Schie, 1998) but a recent meta-anlysis showed that, broadly, prosocial video games are associated with prosocial behaviors (Greitemeyer & Mügge, 2014). Thus, when a game encourages prosocial actions instead of violent ones through rules and feedback, the game is associated with prosocial behaviors outside of the game.

In terms of self-presentation, a recent study found that giving a player control over a character—like in a video game—facilitated a connection between the player and the character (Dillman-Carpentier, Rogers, & Barnard, 2015). The character, in the story, engaged in prosocial, charitable behaviors. After completing the game, players were more likely to visit a website for charity and participate on the site. The study argued that when players had control over the character, the players felt a connection to that character. Thus, the players were more willing to appropriate attributes of the character in the story, in this case, charitable behaviors. Extrapolating from this, video games might encourage prosocial behaviors in the event that the character they are using engages in prosocial behaviors.

Indeed, video games are increasingly complex and some games may be violent and prosocial simultaneously. Different aspects of the game, prosocial or violent, can be made salient through feedback, rules, and self-presentation. This salience impacts whether or not the video game has prosocial outcomes. For example, one person may be playing a *Call of Duty* video game that features a large degree of violence in a war setting. However, the game rules allow for multiplayer modes of play. The idea of socializing and playing with friends might be more salient to this player than committing virtual acts of violence. Similarly, in *Grand Theft Auto V*, a player can commit many criminal acts but the police chase the player whenever he or she does. Likewise, if the player helps the main characters' friends and family, then the plot advances. Thus, the feedback system might make acting prosocially more salient in spite of the player's ability to act in antisocial ways within the game. In fact, Granic and colleagues are "inspired" by the positive possibilities of video games (2014, p. 76) and this perspective should be considered in the larger conversation related to video game play.

REFERENCES

Bandura, A. (2001). Social cognitive theory: An agentic perspective. *Annual Review of Psychology, 52*(1), 1–26.

Bowman, N. D., Kowert, R., & Cohen, E. (2015). When the ball stops, the fun stops too: The impact of social inclusion on video game enjoyment. *Computers in Human Behavior, 53*, 131–139.

Brabham, D. C. (2013). *Crowdsourcing.* Cambridge, MA: MIT Press.

Buckley, K. E., & Anderson, C. A. (2006). A theoretical model of the effects and consequences of playing video games. *Playing Video Games: Motives, Responses, and Consequences,* 363–378.

Chambers, J. H., & Ascione, F. R. (1987). The effects of prosocial and aggressive videogames on children's donating and helping. *The Journal of Genetic Psychology, 148*(4), 499–505.

Colwell, J., Grady, C., & Rhaiti, S. (1995). Computer games, self-esteem and gratification of needs in adolescents. *Journal of Community and Applied Social Psychology,* 5, 195–206.

Dillman-Carpentier, F., Rogers, R., & Barnard, L. (2015). Eliciting behavior from interactive narratives: Isolating the role of agency in connecting with and modeling characters. *Journal of Broadcasting & Electronic Media,* 59(1), 76–93.

Eisenberg, N., Fabes, R. A., & Spinrad, T. L. (2006). Prosocial behaviour. *Handbook of Child Psychology, 3,* 646–718.

Gentile, D. A., Anderson, C. A., Yukawa, S., Ihori, N., Saleem, M., Ming, L. K., & Sakamoto, A. (2009). The effects of prosocial video games on prosocial behaviors: International evidence from correlational, longitudinal, and experimental studies. *Personality and Social Psychology Bulletin.* 35(6) 752–763.

Granic, I., Lobel, A., & Engels, R. C. (2014). The benefits of playing video games. *American Psychologist,* 69(1), 66.

Greitemeyer, T., & Mügge, D. O. (2014). Video games do affect social outcomes a meta-analytic review of the effects of violent and prosocial video game play. *Personality and Social Psychology Bulletin, 40,* 578–589.

Greitemeyer, T., & Osswald, S. (2010). Effects of prosocial video games on prosocial behavior. *Journal of Personality and Social Psychology,* 98(2), 211–221.

Greitemeyer, T., & Osswald, S. (2009). Prosocial video games reduce aggressive cognitions. *Journal of Experimental Social Psychology,* 45(4), 896–900.

Greitemeyer, T., Osswald, S., & Brauer, M. (2010). Playing prosocial video games increases empathy and decreases schadenfreude. *Emotion,* 10(6), 796.

Griffiths, M. D., Davies, M. O., & Chappell, D. (2003). Breaking the stereotype: The case of online gaming. *Cyberpsychology & Behavior,* 6(1), 81–91.

Irvine, M. (2008). Survey: Nearly every American kid plays video games. Usatoday.com. http://usatoday30.usatoday.com/tech/gaming/2008-09-16-american-kids-gamers_N.htm

Ivan, T. (2013). You can now pay to rebuild Curiosity's cube. *computersandvideogames.com.* http://www.computerandvideogames.com/402138/you-can-now-pay-to-rebuild-curiositys-cube/

Liu, Y., Teng, Z., Lan, H., Zhang, X., & Yao, D. (2015). Short-term effects of prosocial video games on aggression: an event-related potential study. *Frontiers in Behavioral Neuroscience, 9.*

Mitchell, E. (1985). The dynamics of family interaction around home video games. *Personal Computers and the Family,* 8, 121–135.

Ostrov, J. M., Gentile, D. A., & Crick, N. R. (2006). Media exposure, aggression and prosocial behavior during early childhood: A longitudinal study. *Social Development,* 15(4), 612–627.

Peskadoshi (2011). Jolly cooperation [Msg 1]. Message posted to http://www.gamefaqs.com/boards/608635-dark-souls/60811013

Penner, L. A., Dovidio, J. F., Piliavin, J. A., & Schroeder, D. A. (2005). Prosocial behavior: Multilevel perspectives. *Annual Review of Psychology,* 56, 365–392.

Prot, S., Gentile, D. A., Anderson, C. A., Suzuki, K., Swing, E., Lim, K. M., & Lam, B. C. P. (2014). Long-term relations among prosocial-media use, empathy, and prosocial behavior. *Psychological Science,* 25(2), 358–368.

Roskos-Ewoldsen, D. R., Roskos-Ewoldsen, B., & Carpentier, F. R. D. (2002). Media priming: A synthesis. *Media Effects: Advances in Theory and Research,* 2, 97–120.

Schie, E. G., & Wiegman, O. (1997). Children and videogames: Leisure activities, aggression, social integration, and school performance. *Journal of Applied Social Psychology,* 27(13), 1175–1194.

Shimai, S., Masuda, K., & Kishimoto, Y. (1990). Influences of TV games on physical and psychological development of Japanese kindergarten children. *Perceptual and Motor Skills*, 70, 771–776.

Slater, M. D. (2003). Alienation, aggression, and sensation-seeking as predictors of adolescent use of violent film, computer and website content. *Journal of Communication*, 53, 105–121.

Slater, M. D., Henry, K. L., Swaim, R. C., & Anderson, L. L. (2003). Violent media content and aggressiveness in adolescents a downward spiral model. *Communication Research*, 30(6), 713–736.

Sneakyø (2013, January 23). A guy giving away 777,000 gold wtf ? [Msg 1]. Message posted to http://eu.battle.net/wow/en/forum/topic/6444145336

Wiegman, O., Kuttschreuter, M., & Baarda, B. (1992). A longitudinal study of the effects of television viewing on aggressive and prosocial behaviours. *British Journal of Social Psychology*, 31(2), 147–164.

Wiegman, O., & Schie, E. G. (1998). Video game playing and its relations with aggressive and prosocial behaviour. *British Journal of Social Psychology*, 37(3), 367–378.

Chapter Four

Mood Management

In the past, a considerable amount of attention has been dedicated to mood management in communication literature (Bryant & Zillmann, 1984; Zillmann, 1988a; Zillmann, 1988b). Traditionally, the mood management paradigm suggests that people consume entertainment media in order to maintain a favorable mood such that people try to maximize the duration and intensity of good moods while minimizing the duration and intensity of bad moods (Zillmann, 1988a; Zillmann, 2000). In other words, a person in a positive mood will choose media that will prolong that mood state. Meanwhile, a person in a negative mood will choose media that repairs that mood. For example, someone who is feeling happy might select to watch a happy movie or post on social media while avoiding a sad documentary in order to maximize his or her positive mood. Conversely, someone who is sad might avoid engaging on social media and instead play a video game to feel productive and competent to repair his or her mood.

Based on existing literature, Zillmann suggests that there are two ways selective exposure, or avoiding certain information while deliberately consuming other information, is used to manage moods:

1. Material is selected that is the opposite valence of the current mood. This would be used to get out of a negative mood.
2. Content is selected that is more gratifying than the current state. This would be used when a mood is positive but could be improved.

As such, critical to mood management theory is selective exposure theory. Zillmann and Bryant (2013) posit that human beings are constantly surrounded by stimuli, so much so that a human being is not capable of processing all of the stimuli at once. Human beings direct their attention toward certain stimuli and not others. Selective exposure then is individuals' perceived ability to control the stimuli around them. Rather than having to decide what to focus on, people create scenarios in which they are only exposed to content they have a predisposition toward. A typical example of this is someone with conservative (or liberal) political beliefs avoiding media messages that conflict with their beliefs by reading/avoiding certain news outlets. Zillmann and Bryant (2013) further suggest that selective exposure can require either very little effort or a large degree of effort. It may be as simple as turning the channel on the television or it might require complete avoidance of certain media platforms. Ultimately, by avoiding or approaching certain messages that fit user preferences, people can alter their moods.

Indeed, mood management theory relies on the notion that environmental factors impact moods and affects (Zillmann, 1988b). As such, the environment must be malleable to the extent that individuals can alter their environments through content selection. For example, the individual can change his or her environment by selecting a romantic comedy over a drama in order to fit his or her current mood state. This alteration of environment to fit mood becomes habitual such that when someone is in a bad mood he or she might be accustomed to putting on a program that is comforting and has proven to be helpful in the past (Zillmann, 1988b). For example, when one is sad, he or she might put on an episode of *Seinfeld* as it helps that person relax and laugh. Fundamentally, this describes a feedback system. The actual mood state is compared to the desired mood state and media is selected. The impact of that media selection is then referenced in order to make future and/or habitual media selections.

Despite the usefulness of mood management in understanding media consumption, two issues that have arisen from this line of inquiry are: explanations of non-hedonic media consumption and the distinction between mood and emotion.

Moods and emotions are closely related concepts, but have some important differences.

Emotions:

- Emotions are *episodic* (Hamm, Schupp, & Weike, 2003) and moods are general mental states that last longer than emotions (Gray & Watson, 2007).
- Emotions tend to be *directional* in that they are the result of a certain stimulus (Hamm et al., 2003).
- Emotions are also *impacted by cognitive factors* (Scherer, 2003). Different appraisals made by participants are shown to predict discrete emotions (Ortony, 1990).

- Similarly, emotions vary in terms of valence, function, and action tendency (Shen & Bigsby, 2010). In other words, emotions are positive or negative, emotions help people adapt to certain stimuli, and emotions result in a certain type of behavior. For example, when someone is afraid, the emotion is negative, its function is to prevent harm, and it encourages revision and reassessment. Meanwhile, someone who is happy is in a positive state in which he or she will attempt to prolong the feeling through self-rewards.

Moods:

- Moods are *broad*, and are not directed at one object (Gray & Watson, 2007).
- Moods are *more frequent* than emotions; in fact, true raw emotions are quite rare but performed emotions are common (Carver & Scheier, 2014; Gray & Watson, 2007).
- Moods tend to be the *aggregate of multiple experiences* (Davidson, 1994).

In summary, moods are general, longer, and not directed at any one thing. Emotions are short and specifically directed at a stimulus. Even though moods and emotions are distinct it is important to understand their differences at the onset and how these difference play into how emotions or moods are managed.

In terms of emotions specifically, Shen and Bigsby (2010) provide a detailed list of discrete emotions and their corresponding action tendencies. This list is not comprehensive but indicative of some of the mood management capabilities of video games.

- When a person is surprised he or she wants to orient him- or herself adequately. A familiar or casual video game might allow a player to reduce this feeling of surprise. This can be accomplished through predictable and orienting feedback as well as easily understood rules.
- When a person is angry he or she wants to remove the obstacle that is making him or her angry. Many games place players in competition so they are allowed to kill other characters or otherwise remove obstacles. If the game is too difficult for the player then it might enhance this anger, as the player would not be able to remove the obstacle. Again, this can be accomplished through game rules and feedback.
- When someone is afraid he or she wants protection from the fear. Video games, as a virtual environment, can provide a safe space without penalty for missteps, or a magic circle.
- When someone feels guilt, he or she implements self-sanctions and strives to reclaim a standard. Maintaining a standard is nearly always a reflection

of a feedback system. As such, games can aid in repairing feelings of guilt, especially if the games allow altruistic actions.

- When someone is happy he or she wants to bask in it and bond with others. Video games, through character interaction and multiplayer modes allow players to prolong and expand their happiness levels.

Meanwhile, mood management theory does an excellent job explaining the use of certain media; however, it tends to focus on positively valenced content. Consider movies like *No Country for Old Men* and books like *The Road*. Both are bleak, brutal, and not necessarily pleasurable. However, *No Country for Old Men* won an Academy Award for best picture and *The Road* won the Pulitzer Prize for fiction. Similarly, within the last year, the news stories that dominated the headlines and broadcasts were the scandals in the NFL, the Ebola outbreak, and the missing Malyasian Airlines flight. These were all sad stories yet many were consuming this content. Mood management theory does not necessarily explain the widespread appeal of this sad and possibly upsetting content.

In order to explore this phenomenon, that people are drawn to negatively valenced content, Oliver (2008) conducted a series of studies examining the consumption of sad movies. In the first study, the prevailing mood state of each participant was assessed then each participant was asked to choose which movie they would prefer to watch from a series of genres. Those who were in a concerned or sympathetic mood were more likely to select a sad movie while those who were not in sad moods preferred comedy movies. In the second study, participants were placed in a hypothetical scenario that promoted a certain mood state. Afterward, the participants ranked their preferences for different movies based on that mood. Those in the concerned or sympathetic mood conditions preferred sad movies while those in the happy condition preferred comedies. The third study replicated study two but revealed that those in a concerned or sympathetic mood state preferred sad movies as well as dramas and romantic films.

In another study exploring mood management as related to non-hedonic media consumption, people renting movies from a video store were asked what their moods were on their way into the store and then reported which movies they rented upon leaving (Strizhakova & Krcmar, 2007). Findings revealed that different emotions were connected to different movie selections. Those who were angry or bored did not select dramas. Those who were aroused selected action movies not dramas. Those who were anxious chose horror movies and those who were sad selected serious films. A similar pattern emerged in a study using mood induction on college students (Greenwood, 2010). Notably, gender appeared to have an impact on these selections. Women tended to prefer romantic movies while men preferred action movies and sad men showed a preference for dark comedies (Greenwood,

2010). An eight-week study of adolescents with depressive disorders revealed that boys were more likely to use media to manage a negative mood state (Dillman Carpentier et al., 2008) and men tended to distract themselves with immersive content more than women (Knobloch-Westerwick, 2007). In the context of news content that may not be strictly pleasurable, Zillmann (2000) suggests that non-hedonic content provides informational utility. This means that people endure unpleasant content in order to acquire information. Thus, non-hedonic media consumption is more deliberate and planned than consumption of hedonic content.

Extrapolating this to video games, this logic may help explain why certain video games are popular even though intuition might indicate that they would not be. At first, it might seem odd that a video game would be popular if it was extremely difficult or if the game focused too much on story. But people might like hard video games if the game provides quality feedback and confers a degree of accomplishment. Also, someone might feel very immersed in a video game story because they feel represented by the character in the game.

Recently a handful of scholars examined how video games can be used for mood management (Oliver et al., 2015). More specifically, the scholars explored how video games, a medium typically associated with "play" and therefore hedonic gratification, might actually be able to provide experiences beyond hedonic gratification. In the first study, participants were asked to recall a particularly fun or a particularly meaningful video game they had played. This revealed that game attributes related to game play were more closely associated with enjoyment while game attributes related to character and story were more closely associated with a meaningful game experience. In light of self-determination theory (Ryan & Deci, 2000), this study found that different elements of a game satisfy different psychological needs. The needs as identified by self-determination theory are competence, autonomy, and relatedness. Quality game play was associated with autonomy and competence. Quality story and characters was associated with feelings of relatedness. The study interpreted this to mean that, even though many games are viewed as hedonic media, video games can provide more profound experiences based on how the game is designed and which attributes are emphasized. A few games that are perhaps emblematic of the meaningful content are: *Heavy Rain*, *The Last of Us*, and *Final Fantasy VII*. Each of these games focuses heavily on narrative and character development. Notably, these elements are typically emphasized by the games' rules and feedback.

Another study examined how the connection to a character in a video game impacts the enjoyment of a video game. Again, participants were asked to recall a particularly fun or a particularly meaningful video game that they had played (Bowman, Rogers, & Sherrick, 2013). As expected, different relationships with the game's character were associated with different manifestations of entertainment. Specifically, when players felt like they had a large degree of control over the character there was increased hedonic enjoyment of the game. Increased feelings of responsibility for a character's well-being were associated with an increased likelihood of having a meaningful experience with that game. This indicates that strong feelings of self-presentation in a game can help predict *how* that game can be used to manage moods. If players are aiming to elicit a more contemplative and less hedonic mood then self-presentation is a key element. The player needs to place him- or herself into the game and experience it firsthand.

In a final study, participants were asked to write a short review of a game that was particularly meaningful or particularly fun (Rogers et al., 2015). These texts were analyzed for common themes. Again, descriptions of fun games tended to focus on aspects of game play while meaningful game descriptions focused on insights into the human condition. For example, fun games were described as challenging, required strategy, or featured realistic game play. On the other hand, meaningful games allowed for connection to characters in the game and difficult moral choices. Thus, different video games can help manage moods when players are looking for a fun experience or a meaningful experience.

While there is not empirical evidence of this, this chapter posits that quality feedback will predict competence, quality rules will predict autonomy, and quality self-presentation will predict feelings of relatedness. As such, these key elements of a video game may fulfill psychological needs that allow players to manage their moods effectively.

REFERENCES

Bowman, N., Rogers, R., & Sherrick, B. (2013). In control or in their shoes? How character attachment differentially influences video game enjoyment and appreciation. Presented at the annual conference of the Broadcast Education Association, Las Vegas, NV.

Bryant, J., & Zillmann, D. (1984). Using television to alleviate boredom and stress: Selective exposure as a function of induced excitational states. *Journal of Broadcasting & Electronic Media, 28*(1), 1–20.

Carver, C., & Scheier, M. (2014). The experience of emotions during goal pursuit. *International Handbook of Emotions in Education,* 56.

Davidson, R. J. (1994). On emotion, mood and related affective constructs. In *The nature of emotion: Fundamental questions*, ed. Paul Ekman and Richard J. Davidson. New York: Oxford University Press.

Dillman Carpentier, F. R., Brown, J. D., Bertocci, M., Silk, J. S., Forbes, E. E., & Dahl, R. E. (2008). Sad kids, sad media? Applying mood management theory to depressed adolescents' use of media. *Media Psychology 11*(1), 143–166.

Gray, E. K., & Watson, D. (2007). Assessing positive and negative affect via self-report. *Handbook of Emotion Elicitation and Assessment,* 171–183.

Greenwood, D. (2010). Of sad men and dark comedies: Mood and gender effects on entertainment media preferences. *Mass Communication & Society,* 13(3), 232–249.

Hamm, A. O., Schupp, H. T., & Weike, A. I. (2003). Motivational organization of emotions: Autonomic changes, cortical responses, and reflex modulation. In R. J. Davidson, K. R.

Scherer, & H. H. Goldsmith (eds.), *The Handbook of Affective Sciences*. Oxford: Oxford University Press.

Knobloch-Westerwick, S. (2007). Gender differences in selective media use for mood management and mood adjustment. *Journal of Broadcasting & Electronic Media*, 51(1), 73–92.

Oliver, M. B. (2008). Tender affective states as predictors of entertainment preference. *Journal of Communication, 58*, 40–61.

Oliver, M., Bowman, N., Woolley, J., Rogers, R., Sherrick, B., & Chung, M.Y. (2015). Video games as meaningful entertainment experiences. *Psychology of Popular Media Culture.*

Ortony, A. (1990). *The cognitive structure of emotions*. Cambridge University Press.

Rogers, R., Woolley, J., Oliver, M., Bowman, N., Sherrick, B. & Chung, M.Y. (2015). Fun versus Meaningful Video Game Experiences: A Qualitative Analysis of User Responses. Presented at the annual conference of the Association for Education in Journalism and Mass Communication, San Francisco, CA.

Ryan, R. M., & Deci, E. L. (2000). Self-determination theory and the facilitation of intrinsic motivation, social development, and well-being. *American Psychologist, 55*(1), 68.

Scherer, K. R. (2003). Introduction: Cognitive components of emotion. In R. J. Davidson, K. R. Scherer, & H. H. Goldsmith (Eds.), *The Handbook of Affective Sciences*. Oxford: Oxford University Press, pp. 563–571.

Shen, L., & Bigsby, E. (2010). Behavioral activation/inhibition systems and emotions: A test of valence vs. action tendency hypotheses. *Communication Monographs, 77*, 1–26.

Strizhakova, Y., & Krcmar, M. (2007). Mood management and video rental choices. *Media Psychology 10*(1), 91–112.

Watson, D. (2000). *Mood and Temperament*. New York: Guilford Press.

Zillmann, D. (1988a). Mood management through communication choices. *American Behavioral Scientist, 31*(3), 327–340.

Zillmann, D. (1988b). Mood management: Using entertainment to full advantage. In L. Donohew, H. E. Sypher, & E. T. Higgins (Eds.), *Communication, social cognition, and affect* (pp. 147–171). Hillsdale, NJ: Erlbaum.

Zillmann, D. (2000). Mood management in the context of selective exposure theory. In M. F. Roloff (Ed.), *Communication yearbook 23* (pp. 103–123). Thousand Oaks, CA: Sage.

Zillmann, D., & Bryant, J. (Eds.). (2013). *Selective exposure to communication*. New York: Routledge.

Chapter Five

History

As mentioned in the education chapter, in one study a participant stated that he learned more about history from the *Call of Duty* video games than he had in any course he had taken (Rogers, 2012). While it has been established that video games can impact the education of history (Egenfeldt-Nielsen, 2005; Lenhart et al., 2008), this sentiment is worth further exploration beyond education. Specifically, this chapter will focus on how video games can effectively portray and recreate history for a variety of benefits.

A video game can place an individual into a historical context. Gee (2008) calls this placement into a historical context, embodied thinking or the "projective stance." Within this "projective stance" the player assumes the role of a character within the game space. In doing so, the player assumes the goals of that character. This is akin to the Proteus effect and the psychological merger discussed earlier in this book (Klimmt, Hefner, & Vorderer, 2009; Lewis, Weber, & Bowman, 2008; Peña, Hancock, & Merola, 2009; Yee & Bailenson, 2007). Further Gee states, "As a player, you must—on the basis of what you learn about the game's story and the game's virtual world— attribute certain mental states (beliefs, values, goals, feelings, attitudes, and so forth) to the virtual character" (2008, p. 258). These attributes then orient the player in that virtual space such that the virtual world and the character's attributes complement one another. Gee uses the example of the video game *Thief* to illustrate this. By playing this game the player embodies the main character and thus obtains the goals and skills of a thief. Based on these parameters, some goals are easier or more difficult to attain. Since the thief is good at hiding, the virtual world is conducive to hiding, such that the character and the world are complementary and exist synergistically. In other words, the world is built to work with or work against the skills of the character/player. Gee is describing how video games can present content in consequential ways based on self-presentation through the character in the virtual world.

The projective stance, in the context of historical video games, is an important notion. Hypothetically, imagine a game that illustrates the civil rights movement in the United States in the 1960s. The game allows the players to embody a variety of characters: a protestor, a politician, Martin Luther King Jr., or Malcolm X. Based on which character the player selects, the player would have different goals as well as different strengths and weaknesses. This would give players a varied and in-depth perspective of historical events based on how the game's self-presentation orients the player within history. For example, if players selected the Martin Luther King Jr. character, they would acquire skills such as being persuasive speakers and they would have peaceful goals. Meanwhile, if players selected the Malcolm X character, they would have violent methods of achieving goals. These differences would impact how the player is experiencing history as recreated in the game.

Continuing the design of a hypothetical game that portrays the civil rights movement in the United States in the 1960s, the game could show the difficulty of and persistence needed for using peaceful means of protest. Thus, the virtual space makes the game's goals more easily achieved through violence, or there are many opportunities for violence that reward the player but work against broad goals. This presentation of the virtual world, in conjunction with the characters included, would allow players to experience the civil rights movement in the United States in the 1960s from a valuable, and challenging, perspective.

The historical experience in video games has been called a living history interaction such that video games sit at the nexus of performance, digital media, and history (Magelssen, 2008). Magelssen (2008), through an example using the Old Sturbridge Village—a living history museum presenting 1830s New England—argues that games allow performance of the virtual past and this helps to clearly establish specifics or details of history. One can observe the way the world functioned at that time as opposed to just hearing it described or reading about it. For example, if a player walks around a virtual version of Old Sturbridge Village he or she can see the flow of people through the city, the details painted on the signs, the patterns of weather, and the expressions on people's faces. This allows for a much richer experience than simply reading a passage in a book.

Besides the historical details and nuances that can be represented by a video game, the video game can offer freedom to the player such that he or she can roam the streets following his or her interests, not dictated by less flexible media. If a player were interested in blacksmithing, he or she could have followed the blacksmith through a daily, monthly, or even yearly routine. In this vein, the game would satisfy dynamic heterogeneity, or the pursuit and test of different hypotheses, as described by Ariely (2000).

Moreover, like the hypothetical game described above, some games allow players to become specific characters in history. *Velvet Assassin* has players assume the role of real-life World War II Special Operations Executive (SOE), Violette Szabo. Similarly, in *The Saboteur*, players use a character based on the real-life William Grover-Williams, another SOE operative in Nazi-occupied France. While both are fictionalized games and designed for entertainment, this allows the player to embody a historical figure and experience historical events in the specific context of a key figure.

While self-presentation is an important factor to consider when discussing video games and history, it is key to note that not all video games have characters for the player to become, or more specifically, characters in a historical context for the player to experience history through the eyes of. For example, in *American Civil War: Gettysburg* players control entire Union or Confederate forces from a God's eye view. Players do not assume the role of a specific character but control a wide range of characters at once in battles like Little Round Top and Pickett's Charge. This is more akin to a player moving pieces around a chess board as opposed to the player *becoming* a piece on the chess board. This sort of presentation, wherein the player assumes a God's eye view, is effective for showing details of specific battles but perhaps not of specific historic individuals.

Games like *Call of Duty 2* allow players to reenact World War II battles from multiple perspectives. Among those featured are: The Russian 13th Guard Rifle Division's fight at Stalingrad, the British 7th Armoured Division in the Second Battle of El Alamein and the Battle of Caen, and the American 2nd Ranger Battalion during the D-Day invasion at Pointe du Hoc. Beyond the presentation of historical events and actual regiments represented at these events, the equipment that players use is rendered to be historically accurate. In fact, some developers go through a large degree of hands-on research to accurately present the sound and feel of the weapons (Plunkett, 2010). The virtual equipment used in these games is designed to replicate the experience of using it as well as having it used against the player. A player can actively experience a virtual version of the Normandy invasion instead of passively experiencing it.

The research and time dedicated to accurate historical representations in video games can be astounding. For the video game *LA Noire*, the developers used old photographs to recreate 1940s Los Angeles (Berstein & Nosowitz, 2011). These photographs not only allowed the game developers to reproduce the architecture of the time but also the conditions of the buildings, construction sites, traffic patterns, and pedestrian congestion. The historical pictures used during game development depicted a real estate boom, which ended up influencing some of the missions/storylines in the game. "As a result, gamers will be immersed in the most accurate version of 1940s Los Angeles ever created" (Berstein & Nosowitz, 2011). Meanwhile the *Assassin's Creed* series attempts to recreate various historical settings such as Masyaf, Jerusalem, Acre, and Damascus during the twelfth century; Venice, Florence, Forli, and San Gimignano, during the fifteenth century renaissance; Colonial America in the eighteenth century and Paris during the French Revolution in the eighteenth century. Video game recreations of history can be so comprehensive that they are used for purposes other than the game. For example, the video game *Brothers in Arms: Road to Hill 30* was used in a History Channel special in order to recreate scenarios from the D-Day invasion in World War II (Sinclair, 2005).

Fullerton (2008) refers to these sorts of games as "documentary games" (p. 215). That is, video games that use a documentary style. Fullerton's piece argues that viewing a simulation is not the same as being inside the simulation and video games offer this opportunity. In *Medal of Honor: Rising Sun* players get to experience a simulation of the attack on Pearl Harbor in the first mission. Fullerton suggests that many of these games take liberties with historical accuracy in order to present the event in a specific way that the game creators wish to emphasize. For example, *Waco Resurrection* is based on the shootout between law enforcement and the Branch Davidians, led by David Koresh, at the Mount Carmel Center near Waco, Texas. The standoff lasted over a month and more than 75 people died (Leppard & Wynick, 2013). On the game's website, the game is described as follows:

> Revisiting the 1993 Waco, Texas, episode, gamers enter the mind and form of a resurrected David Koresh through custom headgear, a voice-activated, hard-plastic 3D skin. Each player enters the network as a Koresh and must defend the Branch Davidian compound against internal intrigue, skeptical civilians, rival Koresh and the inexorable advance of government agents. Ensnared in the custom "Koresh skin", players are bombarded with a soundstream of government "psy-ops", FBI negotiators, the voice of God and the persistent clamor of battle. Players voice messianic texts drawn from the Book of Revelation, wield a variety of weapons from the Mount Carmel cache and influence the behavior of both followers and opponents by radiating a charismatic aura.

Fullerton (2008) suggests that *Waco Resurrection* does not necessarily recreate the events of that standoff but instead uses elements of the game to force players to think about their perspective on the event. Indeed, the game is further described on its website:

> *Waco Resurrection* re-examines the clash of worldviews inherent in the 1993 conflict by asking players to assume the role of a resurrected "cult" leader. It addresses the multi-layered dynamics of a 51-day media-event that served to mobilize the militia movement and radicalize Timothy McVeigh. The game combines elements of subjective documentary with new interactive technolo-

gies to create a visceral gaming experience in which to reconsider the phenomenal possibilities inherent in ideological conflict.

In other words, the game designers use rules to manipulate a player's experience of a historical event in order to create a meaningful experience for the player.

Another game in this category is *Super Columbine Massacre RPG!* (Fullerton, 2008). The game recreates the events of the Columbine High School shooting on April 20, 1999. Players assume the roles of the shooters, Eric Harris and Dylan Klebold. Although many current video games strive for realism in game play and in graphics, *Super Columbine Massacre RPG!* primarily uses cartoonish, pixelated sprites. In response to criticisms, the designer of the game, Danny Ledonne, issued a statement on the game's website where he claimed that his purpose in making the game was to deepen and refine the understanding of the Columbine shooting. Beyond that, the game includes artifacts from the event. Clips of press conferences, real photographs of and lines from the killers' writings are included throughout. Ultimately, the game is a reflection of that day and allows players to think about and engage with the event in a unique way (Fullerton, 2008). The implication then is that the game *should* be offensive. If we are to believe the designer, the game is not intended to simply cash in on a tragedy, instead, its mission is to facilitate understanding of, or at least thought about, the tragedy.

JFK: Reloaded is another game in this tradition. The game recreates the JFK assassination. Players take on the role of the assassin, Lee Harvey Oswald, and are scored based on how accurately they can recreate the actual shooting. As Fullerton (2008) argues, many historical games take liberties with history but *JFK: Reloaded* forces the player to get history right. The stated purpose of this game is to "bring history to life" and test the validity of the Warren Commission, the investigation into JFK's assassination (Press Association, 2004). In fact, the game's purported use is to crowdsource to see all of the different possibilities and "disprove, once and for all, any notion that someone else was involved in the assassination of President Kennedy" (Press Association, 2004). Allowing players to virtually assassinate the president of the United States could be difficult for some to tolerate but upon further inspection, this game may be able to provide closure that other media, such as the Zapruder film, could not.

In *9-11 Survivor*, players find themselves in a burning rendering of the World Trade Center. Outcomes of the game might be dying in the fire, jumping from the building, or escaping to safety. The game designers stated that they made the game to illustrate the devastation of the day and remove the distance between the player and the event (Mirapaul, 2003). While media and photographs were used to accurately recreate the scene, these media do not require the player to *be in* the burning building (Mirapaul, 2003). Many people were profoundly impacted by the World Trade Center attack, but the truth is that many others were not directly impacted. This game allows those with a degree of separation from the event to generate experiences more closely tied to the event.

Fullerton (2008) says that these games put the player in the path of history—a valuable although contentious feature. These video games in particular have been the subject of much controversy. *Super Columbine Massacre RPG!* has been called "insensitive" and "deplorable" (Vargas, 2006). The game was even pulled from a game festival due to its controversial content (Kuchera, 2007). *JFK: Reloaded* has been called despicable (Press Association, 2004) and sickening (Tuohey, 2004). *9-11 Survivor* was criticized for exploiting a tragedy and lacking moral decency (Mirapaul, 2003). In some ways, these criticisms validate the games' stated purposes. Reliving these events should not be easy and enjoyable. To recreate these events is to recreate tragedy, heartbreak, and violence. As a result, if the games did not evoke negative emotions, they would not meet the stated goals of the developers. In other words, the feedback used in these games relates to the emotional experience. In these games, the goal is to engage the player in history. These games are not necessarily about "winning," but instead about presenting a stimulus in order to elicit certain responses. In this way, these games extend feedback beyond the game space and into the space of the player's mental state. This is especially true of a game like *9-11 Survivor*, where the player cannot "win." Instead the player is asked to respond to and consider a series of events presented by the developers.

These video game criticisms are quite common; however, exempt from these criticisms are war games. Games depicting war, like the *Call of Duty* series, are commercially popular and receive little negative attention like the games mentioned above. The harshest piece of criticism found was in an academic source, not a popular press source (Campbell, 2008). In this criticism, it is argued that video games simulate past events like World War II but sanitize them (Campbell, 2008). Campbell (2008) indicates that, in video game versions of history, heroism becomes commonplace and players believe that they understand combat based on these misrepresentations. Ultimately, Campbell suggests that video games have turned World War II into a nostalgic form of play. This is a likely explanation of why war games have received less criticism than games that do not "sanitize" history—games the deliberately leave history intact. This sanitization is achieved through the programming of rules and feedback. In this context, when the rules and feedback do not effectively contest a player's thoughts and feelings, they might be considered sanitized.

Another double standard that emerges is the comparison between video games and movies that portray historical events. *Extremely Loud and Incred-*

ibly Close, a film about 9/11, and *JFK*, a movie about JFK's assassination, were both nominated for Academy Awards for Best Picture. *United 93*, a movie about one of the planes involved in the 9/11 attacks, won many industry awards. *Elephant* and *Bowling for Columbine*, movies addressing the Columbine massacre, were also nominated for numerous awards. What is the reason for this disparity in criticism? This book argues that the disparity is due largely to the fact that game content is interactive and that the player is often placed in the role of a controversial figure.

In summary, what a video game says about history is a confluence of many factors (Perry, 2009). Factors that are critical to this statement are: who the player becomes in history or self-presentation, how the player is oriented in history or feedback/interactivity, and how the player is constrained or rules. The implications of these games may not be readily apparent in this chapter, but how history is presented and experienced can alter the perspective one has on history. This is particularly relevant for events rife with social implications.

REFERENCES

Ariely, D. (2000). Controlling the information flow: Effects on consumers' decision making and preferences. *Journal of Consumer Research, 27*(2), 233–248.

Berstein, J. & Nosowitz, D. (2011). How L.A. Noire rebuilt 1940s Los Angeles using vintage extreme aerial photography. *Popsci.com.* Http://www.popsci.com/technology/article/2011-05/using-extreme-aerial-photography-1920s-rockstar-rebuilt-1940s-los-angeles-la-noire

Campbell, J. (2008). Just less than total war: simulating World War II as ludic nostalgia. In Z. Whalen & l. N. Taylor, (eds.). (2008). *Playing the past: history and nostalgia in video games* (183–200). Nashville: Vanderbilt University Press.

Egenfeldt-Nielsen, S. (2005). *Beyond edutainment: Exploring the educational potential of computer games.* IT University of Copenhagen, Department of Innovation.

Fullerton, T. (2008). Documentary games: Putting the player in the path of history. In Z. Whalen & L. N. Taylor, (Eds.). (2008). *Playing the past: history and nostalgia in video games* (215–238). Nashville: Vanderbilt University Press.

Gee, J. (2008). Video games and embodiment. *Games and Culture. 3*, 253.

Klimmt, C., Hefner, D., & Vorderer, P. (2009). The video game experience as "true" identification: A theory of enjoyable alterations of players' self-perception. *Communication Theory, 19*(4), 351–373.

Kuchera, B. (2007). Super Columbine Massacre RPG pulled from Slamdance competition; the creator speaks with Opposable Thumbs. *Arcs Technica.* Http://arstechnica.com/gaming/2007/01/6534/

Lenhart, A., Kahne, J., Middaugh, E., Macgill, A. R., Evans, C., & Vitak, J. (2008). Teens, video games, and civics: Teens' gaming experiences are diverse and include significant social interaction and civic engagement. *Pew Internet & American Life Project.*

Leppard, B. & Wynick, A. (2013). Waco siege 20 years on: Picture timeline of Texas massacre which killed 76 men, women and children. *Mirror.co.uk.* Http://www.mirror.co.uk/news/world-news/waco-siege-20-years-on-1838748

Lewis, M. L., Weber, R. È., & Bowman, N. D. (2008). They may be pixels, but they're MY pixels:" Developing a metric of character attachment in role-playing video games. *Cyberpsychology & Behavior, 11*(4), 515–518.

Magelssen, S. (2008). Performing the (virtual) past: online character interpretation as living history at Old Sturbridge Village. In Z. Whalen & L. N. Taylor, (Eds.). (2008). *Playing the past: history and nostalgia in video games* (201–214). Nashville: Vanderbilt University Press.

Mirapaul, M. (2003). Online games grab grim reality. *Nytimes.com.* Http://www.nytimes.com/2003/09/17/arts/online-games-grab-grim-reality.html

Peña, J., Hancock, J. T., & Merola, N. A. (2009). The priming effects of avatars in virtual settings. *Communication Research, 36*(6), 838–856.

Perry, N. A. (2009). War and Video Games. University of Rhode Island.

Plunkett, L (2010). Miniguns in the desert: How video game guns are made. *Kotaku.com.* Http://kotaku.com/5625175/miniguns-in-the-desert-how-video-game-guns-are-made

Press Association (2004). JFK shooting game "despicable." *The guardian.com.* Http://www.theguardian.com/technology/2004/nov/22/usnews.games

Rogers, R. (2012). The virtual locker room: Hate speech and online gaming. *Journal of New Media and Culture, 8*(1).

Sinclair, B. (2005). History Channel takes up Brothers in Arms. *Gamespot.com.* Http://www.gamespot.com/articles/history-channel-takes-up-brothers-in-arms/1100-6140685/

Tuohey, J. (2004). JFK Reloaded game causes controversy. *Pcworld.com.* Http://www.pcworld.com/article/118717/article.html?Null

Vargas, J. A. (2006). Shock, anger over Columbine video game. *Washingtonpost.com.* Http://www.washingtonpost.com/wp-dyn/content/article/2006/05/19/AR2006051901979.html

Yee, N., & Bailenson, J. (2007). The Proteus effect: The effect of transformed self-representation on behavior. *Human communication research, 33*(3), 271–290.

Chapter Six

Moral Questions

Similarly to placing players into milestone historical events, video games can also present moral questions to players that they may not readily encounter in the physical world. Broadly, morals are a set of guidelines one uses to guide his or her behavior (Joeckel, Bowman, & Dogruel, 2012). Many video games include moral dilemmas as cornerstones of game play. Consider these examples of moral questions in commercial video games (Goulter, 2011):

- In *Bioshock*, players encounter little girls in the fictional world of Rapture. These girls have a precious resource that helps the player proceed in the game. The player has two options: kill the little girls and get more of the resource immediately or spare the little girls' lives and get only a fraction of that resource instantly. In this fashion, the player must make a short-term sacrifice in order to follow moral guidelines.
- *Grand Theft Auto IV* tells the story of an Eastern European immigrant in the United States, Niko Bellic. Bellic is a veteran of an unnamed war in which he witnessed many atrocities. His military unit was attacked and Bellic was the only survivor. It is revealed that another member of his unit, Darko Brevic, betrayed the unit and had them all killed. Toward the climax of the game, Bellic confronts Brevic. Brevic is a broken man with a severe drug addiction. The player is given the opportunity to kill Brevic or spare his life. This decision impacts the ending of the game that the player will encounter.
- In *Final Fantasy VI*, players come across two characters hanging perilously from a cliff and they can only save one. Who the player chooses to save impacts game play for the remainder of the game.

- In the undercover spy video game, *Splinter Cell: Double Agent*, the player must choose between killing a member of a terrorist cell which results in blown cover or killing a close friend which results in maintaining cover.
- In *Fallout 3*, the player comes across a slave camp known as The Pitt. Many in the town are suffering from an incurable disease. Toward the climax of the mission, players are asked to steal the key ingredient to creating a cure. However, it is revealed that the key to the cure is a human baby. The player must choose whether or not to kidnap the baby in order to come up with a possible cure; asking: is it worth sacrificing the freedom of the one for the good of the many?

Beyond these events, which are arguably supplemental, many video games, such as *Infamous: Second Son*, *Fallout 3*, *Knights of the Old Republic*, and *Mass Effect* use a "morality meter." In these games, players start at a neutral point in terms of being "good" or "bad." If players behave morally then the meter starts to tip in favor of a stereotypical hero or toward "good." If players behave immorally then the meter tips toward a renegade or rebel type of character, or "bad." For example, in *Infamous: Second Son*, the player often battles enemy soldiers. If the player uses lethal force and kills enemies and civilians, that is considered immoral and the gauge tips in that direction. If the player subdues the enemy without killing him or her, this is considered moral and the gauge tips in the other direction. Notably, the immediate outcome is the same in either case: The enemy is incapacitated but the feedback is intended to make the player feel that they are doing "good" or "bad."

Morally complex video games or games that use morality as a narrative theme and gameplay device are fairly common. One video game company, Telltale Games, uses complex moral decisions as a primary video game mechanic. On their website they describe their games as: "adventure games focused on story and characters. . . driven by the choices that *you* make: we see you as the final collaborator in telling the story of the game." One of their games, *The Walking Dead*, won more than 90 game of the year awards in 2012 despite it being more of an "interactive drama" than a video game (Welsh, 2012). The game forces players into complex, morally ambiguous scenarios such as choosing to help one character over another or performing mercy killings. For key decisions in the game, summary screens share statistics among the game's community showing how many people chose which options. Surprisingly, more often than not, people chose the moral, rather than the immoral, option. According to the games' website, these moral choices include:

- When one erratic character suffers from a heart attack, players have the choice to help resuscitate him or kill him off. Sixty-nine percent of the players tried to resuscitate him despite the risk his survival posed.
- Cannibals capture the main character and his group. Upon escape the player has the choice to kill or spare one of the cannibals/captors and 82 percent chose to spare him.
- The main character is bitten by a zombie, which will turn him into a zombie eventually and put the rest of the group in peril. The player has the option to be honest with the rest of the group of survivors about the bite or to hide the bite from the group. Eighty percent of players chose to be honest with the group.
- There were times when the stats were more evenly distributed. For example, when given the opportunity to steal supplies, 55 percent of players did so.

This raises an interesting question: When video games allow players to do deplorable things, how are those decisions made and what are the implications of those decisions? Might the opportunity to make a moral decision—even a negative one—provide some social value to the player? What follows is a review of literature on morality and media consumption.

Character morality has been theorized to play a major role in media enjoyment. Indeed, disposition theory suggests that audience members enjoy content more when a "good guy" is rewarded and a "bad guy" is punished (Raney, 2015; Zillmann, 1996). In other words, audience members enjoy content that relies on notions of justice and morality (Raney, 2006; Zillmann, 1991). Zillmann (1996) argues that early in the process of media consumption, like the start of a movie, audience members judge whether or not a character is moral. The audience member will have a positive or negative disposition toward that character and will likely root for the "good guy" and against the "bad guy." Based on how the story ends, the audience member will feel a certain way about the media content. In this fashion, Zillman (2000) refers to audience members "untiring moral monitors" constantly assessing how characters should and should not be acting based on the audience members' moral beliefs. Comparably, Raney (2015) argues that perceptions of morality regulate how much a person likes a character, reacts to the character's challenges, and the story ending.

Not surprisingly, the morals that one person views as salient can help predict what sort of content he or she consumes (Bowman, Joeckel, & Dogruel, 2012); meaning that most people select media content that matches their moral beliefs. Notably, different groups can have different moral beliefs (Tamborini et al., 2013). For example, political liberals tend to value morals related to harm/care and fairness/reciprocity, while political conservatives value harm/care, fairness/reciprocity, in-group/loyalty, authority/respect, and

purity/sanctity (Haidt & Graham, 2007). Similarly, differences in moral salience have been demonstrated between nationalities with video games. One
study examined differences between American and German adolescents in a
virtual environment when confronted with violations of morality (Joeckel,
Bowman, & Dogruel, 2013). The results showed that the German participants were less likely to violate a moral when that moral was salient. However, the American adolescents appeared to violate these morals randomly. A
similar study was performed with elderly Americans and elderly Germans
(Dogruel, Joeckel, & Bowman, 2013). The German participants found more
of the moral modules less salient than their American counterparts and therefore were more likely to violate a moral scenario. In these cases, morality
salience varied based on age and nationality. Differences among other demographic groups should be expected as well.

Moral judgments have mostly been explained through reasoning, but people often rely on their intuition when making a moral judgment (Graham,
Haidt, & Nosek, 2009; Haidt, 2001). Empirical research supports this as the
salience of specific morals predicted perceptions of character morality, and
then perceived character morality predicted less appeal of a narrative when a
"bad guy" received a reward (Tamborini et al., 2013). In other words, if an
audience member's moral salience predicted how he or she felt about a
character, then how he or she felt about a character impacted perceptions of
how that character was treated. Meanwhile, Tamborini's (2011) Model of
Intuitive Morality and Exemplars (MIME), suggests that exposure to media
and an individual's cultural environment impact the salience of certain moral
modules. This, in turn can lead to either automatic appraisal of morals or a
rationalized appraisal of morals. The MIME accounts for both short and
long-term effects that may result from repeated exposure to certain media
content. Increased moral salience leads to fewer violations of that moral
while decreased moral salience leads to satisficing or compromising morals
(Joeckel et al., 2012). This suggests that if a game cues moral salience then
morals are part of the decision-making process within the game. If the game
does not cue moral salience then the easiest option is selected, not necessarily
the moral one.

While many video games include violence, theft, and other antisocial
actions, players of video games might actually be playing according to the
feel of the game rather than thinking about the moral implications of their
choices (Hartmann, 2011). People are compelled to follow their moral intuitions, but within a video game space those morals might not be relevant
(Joeckel, et al., 2012). Thus, concern over moral violations in video games
might be overblown (Joeckel et al., 2012). In other words, a video game
might emphasize high scores instead of morals. In that game, there should be
fewer moral choices from players than if it emphasized story.

Another possible explanation of these antisocial behaviors in games is that players are morally disengaged from the actions in the game. People find ways to morally disengage from stimuli they find unpleasant (Bandura, 1999; Moore, Detert, Klebe Treviño, Baker, & Mayer, 2012). Raney (2004, 2015) suggests that becoming morally disengaged with entertainment media can be pleasurable for some. Further, moral disengagement may be necessary to enjoy certain media that include immoral behaviors that would otherwise upset audience members. For example, Quentin Tarantino and Martin Scorcese movies are ultra-violent and include many immoral activities. In order to enjoy these movies, and many people do according to reviews, audience members may need to participate in moral disengagement.

In violent video games, players often might engage in moral management in order to enjoy the game (Klimmt, Schmid, Nosper, Hartmann, & Vorderer, 2006). Rather than focusing on violence, players focus on the fact that the game is not "real" and focus on winning a competition. In this way, video games might actually cue moral disengagement (Hartmann & Vorderer, 2010). If a game's story justifies violence or if the game play requires acts of violence to progress, then a player can morally disengage from the acts he or she is committing within the game. Another study supports this proposition. When someone was more familiar with a violent video game or viewed it as "just a game" they did not have as much negative effect when committing acts of violence in the game (Hartmann & Vorderer, 2010).

Importantly, many video games do not pose moral questions regardless of their content. For example, in *Space Invaders*, the player kills legions of enemies but it is not likely to increase moral salience because the graphics are rudimentary, the plot is science fiction, and the game play is engaging. Blowing up alien space ships does not conjure up ambiguous ethics. Instead, pursuing the high score is highlighted. When graphical fidelity is increased in video games and the narrative calls attention to the players' actions, morality will likely become much more salient. For example, *Spec Ops: The Line* is a first-person military shooter designed to challenge and examine acts of violence. As such, it should be expected that players are engaging with *Spec Ops: The Line* on a deeper level than pure entertainment. Instead, players might be having meaningful experiences with this game when they involve moral decisions (Oliver et al., 2015).

Finally, moral choices in video games could actually have a noteworthy impact on players. When people playing a video game committed acts of violence that were not justified, they felt guilty (Hartmann, Toz, & Brandon, 2010). This guilt can lead to increased moral sensitivity (Grizzard, Tamborini, Lewis, Wang, & Prabhu, 2014). Thus, constructs of the game can actually induce moral responses.

These moral outcomes seem to be the interaction of many different concepts: game narrative, game play, the Proteus effect, and personal feelings.

As a result, it is very difficult to diagnose and explore. Furthermore, much of the literature detailed above runs in opposition to the Computers as Social Actors (CASA) paradigm (Reeves & Nass, 1996). Under the CASA paradigm, computers—and the interactions therein—are treated like real people. Young (2013) similarly argues against the justification for immoral action in video games. Specifically, Young states that there is a double standard for justifying immoral video game content. For example, one might kill many people in a video game without giving it much thought but one would be very hesitant to commit a taboo act such as pedophilia in a video game. This paradox does not make sense to Young. However, this disparity might be explained through the notion that the morality salience of pedophilia is not as easily subdued as the morality salience of violence.

Also, many of the moral choices in video games have been called "ludicrous" such that they are more or less inconsequential and have no real impact on the game (Sheridan, 2014). In *Fable*, the player is asked to kill his or her sister in order to create a powerful weapon but this decision takes place after the game's final battle, removing the need for a more powerful weapon. In *Bioshock Infinite* players are given the opportunity to abuse/degrade a mixed race couple or abstain from doing so but the outcome is the same regardless of the choice; therefore the moral choice is inconsequential in terms of the game play and narrative progress.

Given the debate surrounding the complexity of morality in video games, this book suggests that observing the rules, feedback, and self-presentation of a video game will highlight the issue more clearly. First, moral codes are understood as rules. The type of moral a game asks a player to breach is determined by the game rules and will differ in salience depending on the audience member. Beyond that, game rules, by definition, either allow for moral transgressions or not. If moral transgressions are allowed then the players' reaction to moral transgressions or moral compliance will be driven by the type of feedback the player receives for upholding or breaking moral codes. In that vein, feedback can emphasize narrative or game play in order to enforce moral decisions. Lastly, the more a player feels connected to the character, the more he or she will feel moral salience for that character. Indeed, Lewis, Weber, and Bowman (2008) found that players tend to feel *responsible* for their characters when they feel connected to them. This should include making ethical decisions that comply with the character's/player's perspective and interests.

Video games get a lot of attention for allowing players to perform immoral actions, among other things (McKernan, 2013). Yet there may be value in allowing players a safe virtual space to perform these behaviors. Similarly, games that allow immoral behaviors sell well—at the time this was written a majority of the games on the best seller list allowed immoral behaviors—

suggesting that exploring complex moral questions is something that video game players enjoy and will spend money on.

REFERENCES

Bandura, A. (1999). Moral disengagement in the perpetration of inhumanities. *Personality and Social Psychology Review, 3*(3), 193–209.

Bowman, N. D., Joeckel, S., & Dogruel, L. (2012). A question of morality? The influence of moral salience and nationality on media preferences. *Communications: The European Journal of Communication Research, 37*(4), 345–369.

Dogruel, L., Joeckel, S., & Bowman, N. D. (2013). Elderly people and morality in virtual worlds: A cross-cultural analysis of elderly people's morality in interactive media. *New Media & Society, 15*(2), 276–293.

Goulter, T. (2011). Gaming's most difficult decisions. *Gamesradar.com.* http://www.gamesradar.com/gamings-most-difficult-decisions/?page=3

Graham, J., Haidt, J., & Nosek, B. A. (2009). Liberals and conservatives rely on different sets of moral foundations. *Journal of Personality and Social Psychology, 96*(5), 1029.

Grizzard, M., Tamborini, R., Lewis, R. J., Wang, L., & Prabhu, S. (2014). Being bad in a video game can make us morally sensitive. *Cyberpsychology, Behavior, and Social Networking, 17*(8), 499–504.

Haidt, J. (2001). The emotional dog and its rational tail: A social intuitionist approach to moral judgment. *Psychological Review, 108,* 814–834.

Haidt, J., & Graham, J. (2007). When morality opposes justice: Conservatives have moral intuitions that liberals may not recognize. *Social Justice Research, 20*(1), 98–116.

Hartmann, T. (2011). Users' experiential and rational processing of virtual violence. In K. Poels & S. Malliet (Eds.), *Vice city virtue: Moral issues in digital game play* (pp. 135–150). Leuven, Belgium: Acco.

Hartmann, T., Toz, E., & Brandon, M. (2010). Just a game? Unjustified virtual violence produces guilt in empathetic players. *Media Psychology, 13*(4), 339–363.

Hartmann, T., & Vorderer, P. (2010). It's okay to shoot a character: Moral disengagement in violent video games. *Journal of Communication, 60*(1), 94–119.

Joeckel, S., Bowman, N. D., & Dogruel, L. (2012). Gut or game? The influence of moral intuitions on decisions in video games. *Media Psychology, 15*(4), 460–485.

Joeckel, S., Bowman, N. D., & Dogruel, L. (2013). The Influence of Adolescents' Moral Salience on Actions and Entertainment Experience in Interactive Media. *Journal of Children and Media, 7*(4), 480–506.

Klimmt, C., Schmid, H., Nosper, A., Hartmann, T., & Vorderer, P. (2006). How players manage moral concerns to make video game violence enjoyable. *Communications, 31*(3), 309–328.

Lewis, M. L., Weber, R. È., & Bowman, N. D. (2008). "They may be pixels, but they're MY pixels": Developing a metric of character attachment in role-playing video games. *Cyberpsychology & Behavior, 11*(4), 515–518.

McKernan, B. (2013). The Morality of Play Video Game Coverage in The New York Times From 1980 to 2010. *Games and Culture, 8*(5), 307–329.

Moore, C., Detert, J. R., Klebe Treviño, L., Baker, V. L., & Mayer, D. M. (2012). Why employees do bad things: Moral disengagement and unethical organizational behavior. *Personnel Psychology, 65*(1), 1–48.

Oliver, M., Bowman, N., Woolley, J., Rogers, R., Sherrick, B. & Chung, M. Y. (in press). Video games as meaningful entertainment experiences. *Psychology of Popular Media Culture.*

Raney, A. A. (2004). Expanding disposition theory: Reconsidering character liking, moral evaluations, and enjoyment. *Communication Theory, 14*(4), 348–369.

Raney, A. A. (2006). The psychology of disposition-based theories of media enjoyment. In J. Bryant & P. Vorderer (Eds.), *Psychology of entertainment* (pp. 137–150). Mahwah, NJ: Lawrence Erlbaum Associates.

Raney, A. A. (2015). The role of morality in emotional reactions to and enjoyment of media entertainment. *Journal of Media Psychology 23*(1), 18–23.

Reeves, B., & Nass, C. (1996). *How people treat computers, television, and new media like real people and places*. CSLI Publications and Cambridge University Press.

Sheridan, C. (2014). Gaming's most ludicrous moral choices. *Gamesradar.com.* http://www.gamesradar.com/gamings-most-ludicrous-moral-choices/?utm_source=zergnet.com&utm_medium=referral&utm_campaign=zergnet_329438

Tamborini, R. (2011). Moral intuition and media entertainment. *Journal of Media Psychology: Theories, Methods, and Applications, 23*(1), 39.

Tamborini, R., Eden, A., Bowman, N. D., Grizzard, M., Weber, R., & Lewis, R. J. (2013). Predicting media appeal from instinctive moral values. *Mass Communication and Society, 16*(3), 325–346.

Welsh, O. (2012). The Walking Dead review. *Eurogamer.net.* http://www.eurogamer.net/articles/2012-11-22-the-walking-dead-review

Young, G. (2013). Enacting taboos as a means to an end; but what end? On the morality of motivations for child murder and paedophilia within gamespace. *Ethics and Information Technology, 15*(1), 13–23.

Zillmann, D. (2000). Basal morality in drama appreciation. In I. Bondebjerg (Ed.), *Moving images, culture, and the mind* (pp. 53–63). Luton: University of Luton Press.

Zillmann, D. (1991). Empathy: Affect from bearing witness to the emotions of others. In J. Bryant & D. Zillmann (Eds.), *Responding to the screen: Reception and reaction processes* (pp. 135–167). Hillsdale, NJ: Lawrence Erlbaum Associates.

Zillmann, D. (1996). The psychology of suspense in dramatic exposition. In P. Vorderer, W. J. Wulff, & M. Friedrichsen (Eds.), *Suspense: conceptualizations, theoretical analyses, and empirical explorations* (pp 199–231). Mahwah, NJ: Lawrence Erlbaum Associates.

III

The Negative

Chapter Seven

Violence

There is no disputing it: Video games have a violent tradition. The mere mention of *Grand Theft Auto* conjures thoughts of car-jackings and the murder of prostitutes. Even some of the earliest video games ever made were violent. The 1975 video game, *Gun Fight*, featured western-style shootouts. The 1978 hit *Space Invaders* required players to shoot and kill hordes of aliens. In *Tank*, players fought to the death using the eponymous vehicles. Many video games contain violence because games force players to overcome an obstacle; one common form of this is conflict or defeating an enemy (Yenigun, 2013). Furthermore, violent games are popular (Yenigun, 2013) so companies are motivated to produce them.

A series of content analyses show that video games have contained violence for many years. A content analysis of Nintendo and Sega Genesis—platforms popular in the late 1980s and early 1990s—video games revealed that 80 percent of the games analyzed included violence with half of the games including violence directed at an other (Dietz, 1998). Only 27 percent of the games contained socially acceptable aggression, like violence in a sports game. In another content analysis of video games on the Nintendo 64, Sega Dreamcast, and Sony Playstation, consoles popular in the mid to late 1990s, showed that mature video games often featured justified acts of graphic gun violence (Smith, Lachlan, & Tamborini, 2003) but a study of E (everyone) rated games using a comparable sample revealed that 64 percent of the games included violence (Thompson & Haninger, 2001). Violence in these games for "everyone" made up nearly a third of the playtime of each game on average. Beyond that, the player was *required* to commit violence or *rewarded* for committing violence in 60 percent of the games. Taken in conjunction, games approved for children are violent but mature games are that much *more* violent. Similarly, a content analysis of mid-2000s top-selling games indicated that 60 percent of video games included violence as a major component (Dill, Gentile, Richter, & Dill, 2005). Since the consensus is that video games are violent, a more recent content analysis on this topic examined the nature of violence in video games (Hartmann, Krakowiak, & Tsay-Vogel, 2014). In summary, there is plenty of evidence that violence is common in video games.

As mentioned in the opening section of this book, video games are linked to acts of "real" world violence. The shootings at Columbine High School and Sandy Hook Elementary School as well as the Norway shootings were all linked to video game play (Brown, 1999; Ferguson, 2013; Pidd, 2012). Violence is perhaps the most prominent social issue related to video games. Even the Supreme Court of the United States weighed in on this debate in *Brown v. Entertainment Merchants Association* (formerly known as *Schwarzenegger v. Entertainment Merchants Association*). In this case, California put forth a statute that prohibited the sale of violent video games to minors. The law also required that video games use a state-run labeling system to inform consumers as to what violent content the game contained. Meanwhile, the video game industry argued that this law was a violation of the First Amendment. This debate has been ongoing since video games entered the mainstream in the 1970s (Williams, 2003). In 2005 alone there were more than 60 bills proposed to regulate video games in the United States (Sweeting, 2005). Notably, none of these regulations were upheld in the United States. Given the volume and frequency of bills intended to regulate video games, the Supreme Court's decision provides a degree of closure on the issue. Ultimately, the Supreme Court ruled against the statute banning the sale of violent video games to minors as it was ruled a violation of the First Amendment. However, it is worth mentioning that the author of the decision, Justice Scalia, was careful to note that the Court's decision was based on legal precedent, *not* if violent games should or should not be played by minors (for further exploration of the ethics of this ruling see Rogers, in press). This decision also introduces a paradox in regulation as children are not afforded access to sexual content but they are afforded access to violent content, an issue the Court is explicitly aware of. Thus, the question becomes, how can children be adequately protected from harmful violent content without infringing upon the First Amendment rights of others?

While violent video game play is legal for minors in the United States, minors do not have the same access to violent video games worldwide. For example, Germany has banned *Dead Rising 3* and Brazil banned *Bully* (Reed, 2014). In Switzerland, a law was passed that completely banned violent video games (MCV, 2010). These bans are justified by arguments suggesting that video game violence can result in: desensitization toward violence, emotional distress, and, most of all, encouraging violent behaviors.

When discussing how video games might cause violence it is critical to clearly establish how violence is defined. Anderson and Bushman (2001) state that violence is an acute form of aggression like physical attacks. More broadly, aggression refers to an action intended to harm someone who does not willfully receive the harm (Anderson & Bushman 2001). Intention is critical to aggression. If someone is killed accidentally, that is not considered aggressive but if someone throws a punch at another and no one is hurt because the punch was poorly aimed, that is considered aggression. Aggressive behaviors might include things like physically attacking another person, yelling at another person, or insulting another person. Notably, distinctions are made for aggressive thought and aggressive affect such that one might have thoughts to harm another or one might experience an emotion that is aggressive (Anderson & Bushman, 2001; Anderson et al., 2010). In yet another study, aggression is examined in terms of behaviors, cognition, affect, decreased empathy, and physical arousal (Anderson et al., 2010).

Many studies on video games and violence focus on aggression, not violence specifically. Even so, aggression has been parsed further. One study examined aggressive dialogue in video games (Ivory, Williams, Martins, & Consalvo, 2009). In this study, the frequency of the "seven dirty words" (shit, piss, fuck, cunt, cocksucker, motherfucker, and tits) was coded as well as mild profanity (damn, hell) and other words that could be considered aggressive (bitch). In another study, aggression was discussed in terms of harassment between game players such that they would call each other "faggot" and "nigger" (Rogers, 2012). One study examined arousal via skin conductance and aggressive thoughts as related to violent video game play (Ivory & Kalyanaraman, 2007). This study posited that when someone was highly aroused, this heightened state could lead to excitation transfer, or the idea that arousal from one event could be carried over into an unrelated event (Zillmann, 1971). This means that if a person has heightened arousal as a result of playing a violent video game, this heightened arousal could be carried over to non game-related scenarios. In doing so, the likelihood of aggression is increased. Likewise, if a video game increases aggressive thoughts, this suggests that aggression has been primed (Roskos-Ewoldsen, Roskos-Ewoldsen, & Carpentier, 2002). Indeed, Anderson and colleagues suggest that the effects of exposure to video game violence in the short term can be explained by priming (Anderson et al., 2010).

In light of the vast complexity of violent video games, the General Aggression Model (GAM, comparable to the GLM discussed in the education chapter) combines several existing theories of aggression and allows for multiple explanations of aggression (Anderson & Bushman, 2002). The GAM focuses on the "person in the situation," "consisting of one cycle of an ongoing social interaction" (Anderson & Bushman, 2002, p. 34). The model accounts for: individual characteristics as well as the individual's internal state, situational context, and appraisal/decision processes. Personal traits and environmental characteristics are considered inputs. Features of the person include things such as his or her personality, gender, beliefs, and values. Environmental features include things such as aggression primes, provocation (insults, threats, etc.), frustration, and pain. Video games could be considered an environmental factor. According to the GAM, the features of a person and the features of the situation create an internal state. Internal states are broken down into three categories: cognitive, affect, and arousal. These features might make aggressive cognitions more accessible, they might put someone in a bad mood, or elicit an emotion more prone to aggression. The features may lead to high arousal, which can then be transferred to another situation. Consider these examples: A person at a football game might be excited by a close game that is decided in the final moments. Then this fan overreacts to a frustrating traffic jam after the game. Or a person walking out of a violent action movie might be more likely to have aggressive cognitions than a person walking out of a romantic film.

The internal state of a person impacts how he or she evaluates a scenario. Initial appraisals are automatic. Anderson and Bushman (2002) offer an example of this: Person 1 bumps into person 2 who has aggressive cognitions. Person 2, with aggressive thoughts, is more likely to perceive the bump as an aggressive act. Meanwhile, a third person with non-aggressive thoughts would more likely perceive the bump to be an accident. Depending on available resources, such as cognitive capacity, a person will reevaluate his or her initial appraisal of a situation. Reevaluation results in thoughtful action while relying on immediate appraisal can result in impulsive action, aggressive or otherwise. In the above example with aggressive person 2, if he or she was depleted of cognitive resources he or she would be more likely to strike person 1. If person 2 had the cognitive resources, he or she would likely rethink striking person 1 and ask for an apology. In sum, the GAM tries to provide an understanding of the factors that predict aggressive and nonaggressive behaviors.

Due to the wide range of conceptualizations and operationalizations of aggression, it should be no surprise that much of the research on video games and violence is inconsistent. Many studies have come to opposing conclusions. While the preponderance of evidence indicates that exposure to violent video games is related to aggression, some others suggest that there is not such a strong relationship between the two.

STUDIES THAT INDICATE THERE IS NOT A STRONG CONNECTION BETWEEN VIOLENT VIDEO GAME PLAY AND AGGRESSION

Research conducted with college students indicated that more in-game violence did not lead to an increase in aggressive affect (Scott, 1995). The author argues that this directly opposes the perspective that video game violence causes players to feel aggression. Another experiment had participants play a highly aggressive game, a mildly aggressive game, or they were placed in a no game condition (Anderson & Ford, 1986). In this study, playing a video game resulted in more hostility but there was no significant difference between the highly aggressive game and the mildly aggressive game. While those studies are quite dated, in yet another more recent study, exposure to violent video games and previous play of violent video games predicted no difference in aggression (Ferguson et al., 2008). In a follow-up correlational study, predisposition toward aggression, violence in the family, and gender all predicted aggression, but play of violent video games did not (Ferguson et al., 2008). A final study examined the intersection of violent video games and technological advancement, as participants were placed into one of four conditions: non-violent old game, non-violent new game, violent old game, and non-violent new game (Ivory & Kalyanaraman, 2007). Aggression was measured in three ways: aggressive thoughts, aggressive affect, and arousal. There were no significant effects of technological advancement or violence on aggressive thoughts nor did technological advancement predict aggressive affect. However, violence marginally predicted feelings of hostility though the authors caution against putting too much weight on this tenuous finding. Measured through skin conductance and self-report measures, arousal was impacted by newer games but not by violent games. In this fashion, the technology was assumed to impact aggression in terms or arousal, not violence.

STUDIES PROVIDING EVIDENCE THAT VIOLENT VIDEO GAMES DO LEAD TO AGGRESSION

A study involving elementary school students showed that exposure to video game violence was associated with children's lowered feelings of empathy but other media violence did not have the same impact nor did exposure to real-life violence (Funk, Baldacci, Pasoldm, & Baumgardner, 2004). This study argued that the interactive nature of video games is a likely explanation of their findings. In another study, correlational data revealed that aggressive and delinquent behaviors were both linked to violent video game play (Anderson & Dill, 2000). Players of violent video games also tended to have more aggressive personalities. Further, higher rates of video game play were associated with aggressive behavior. Importantly, these relationships were correlational, not causal. This means the researchers cannot conclude that aggression was the result of playing the violent video games. Indeed, the inverse might be accurate or a third factor may be at play with both. Consequently, Anderson and Dill (2000) performed an experiment to establish whether or not video game violence *causes* aggression. In this experiment, participants played a violent video game (*Wolfenstein 3D*) or a non-violent video game (*Myst*). Those who played the violent video game displayed more aggressive behavior toward human opponents than those who played the nonviolent video game. Aggressive behavior was operationalized through a noise punishment. Participants could set the duration and volume level of the noise punishment that their opponents would receive. Those playing the violent game were more aggressive in administering noise punishments to their opponents than those playing the non-violent game (Anderson & Dill, 2000). In a similar study, participants were allowed to set the noise levels that their opponent had to endure (Bartholow & Anderson, 2002). Participants played a violent (*Mortal Kombat*) or a non-violent video game (*PGA Tournament Golf*). After playing the video game, participants competed with a confederate in a reaction time task and the loser received a blast of white noise. Participants who played the violent video game set the noise punishment at higher volumes than those playing the non-violent video game.

Given the conflicting studies, it is worthwhile to examine meta-analyses on violent video games. Three meta-analyses by Ferguson have argued that the effects of violent video games have been overblown (Ferguson, 2007a, 2007b; Ferguson & Kilburn, 2009). A fourth meta-analysis showed that there was a relationship between video game play and aggression but the relationship between video games and aggression was smaller than the relationship between television exposure and aggression (Sherry, 2001). However, a series of meta-analyses from another scholar, Anderson, show that exposure to violent video games does *definitively* impact aggression. A meta-analysis of 33 tests showed that violent video games increase aggression across gender and age groups (Anderson & Bushman, 2001). Importantly, these effects seemed to only last for a short period of time and they were more pronounced when the target of the violence was not a human. Similarly, violent video games predicted aggressive thoughts, emotions, and arousal. In yet another meta-analysis, playing violent video games predicted aggression (thoughts, emotions, and behaviors) and studies with more appropriate methods yield larger effect sizes (Anderson, 2004). In a more recent meta-analysis Anderson and colleagues (2010) demonstrated that exposure to violent video games was associated with aggressive behaviors, thoughts, affect, decreased sympathy, and physical arousal. Importantly, these results were found regardless of sex, culture, and age. Moreover, Anderson and colleagues (2010) point out shortcomings with the Ferguson meta-analyses that indicate that violent video game's relationship to aggression is overstated. Anderson and colleagues (2010) state plainly that violent video game play poses a causal risk for aggression.

Given the large degree of evidence that violent video games can cause aggression, the remainder of this chapter will be dedicated to exploring possible explanations as to *how* violent video games might cause aggression. In their meta-analysis, Anderson and colleagues (2010) suggest that short-term exposure to violent video games can prime aggression in a variety of forms. Meanwhile, repeated exposure to video game violence can have long-term effects such that the player's attitudes and expectancies related to violence will shift.

Funk and colleagues (2004) argue that interactivity is another possible explanation as to why violent video games might be particularly impactful. While there is not much evidence to support this claim, extrapolating research on self-presentation offers deeper understanding of this perspective. In many video games, the player is the one committing the act of violence or the one being attacked. Thus, the player reacts as if he or she is the one being attacked or doing the attacking. More clarity on this point would help to define which video games impact aggression and which do not. If the player commits no violence, then according to the self-presentation literature, the effects should be blunted. If the player commits violence, then the effects should be expanded. These factors, as related to self-presentation and interactivity, might help explain some of the inconsistencies found between studies.

Expanding on interactivity, the GAM (Anderson & Bushman, 2002) can be understood as a feedback loop. The inputs, environmental and personal, are entered into the loop. Then the outcome and subsequent social interaction should reshape the inputs. This is especially true of environmental stimulus. If a person has an unpleasant aggressive social encounter, then he or she can adjust his or her media consumption or style of video game play in order to alter future outcomes. In any case, video game play can be used to alter feelings of aggression in a circular system.

Another aspect worth considering is how the rules and feedback encourage or discourage violence. For example, in the video game *Bulletstorm* players are encouraged to "kill with skill." Players are awarded points for each kill and they earn more points for creative and elaborate kills like launching, bounding with a chain, exploding, or impaling an enemy on a drill. Meanwhile in *Fallout 3*, if a player kills certain characters, he or she will be treated as an enemy and attacked on sight by others in the game. This reward or punishment system likely contributes to how attitudes toward aggression are shaped during play. Indeed, Anderson and colleagues (2010) state that social-cognitive models of aggression help us understand this issue. Furthermore, even though *Bulletstorm* is extremely violent, it is also not realistic. The weapons are fictional and the gore is deliberately overdone. The realism of the space in which the game takes place and the role of violence within that world likely alters perceptions of violence and aggression as well.

In conclusion, games could be developed that discourage violence and present worlds in which violence does not have a meaningful role, which should help impact attitudes toward aggression. Much of the literature has used excitation transfer, social cognitive theory, and priming as theoretical frameworks and a more thorough understanding of the impact of video game violence can be achieved through self-presentation, rules, and feedback.

REFERENCES

Anderson, C. A. (2004). An update on the effects of playing violent video games. *Journal of Adolescence*, *27*(1), 113–122.

Anderson, C. A., & Bushman, B. J. (2001). Effects of violent video games on aggressive behavior, aggressive cognition, aggressive affect, physiological arousal, and prosocial behavior: A meta-analytic review of the scientific literature. *Psychological Science*, *12*(5), 353–359.

Anderson, C. A., & Bushman, B. J. (2002). Human aggression. *Psychology*, *53*(1), 27.

Anderson, C. A., & Dill, K. E. (2000). Video games and aggressive thoughts, feelings, and behavior in the laboratory and in life. *Journal of Personality and Social Psychology*, *78*(4), 772.

Anderson, C. A., & Ford, C. M. (1986). Affect of the game player: Short-term effects of highly and mildly aggressive video games. *Personality and Social Psychology Bulletin*, *12*(4), 390–402.

Anderson, C. A., Shibuya, A., Ihori, N., Swing, E. L., Bushman, B. J., Sakamoto, A., & Saleem, M. (2010). Violent video game effects on aggression, empathy, and prosocial behavior in eastern and western countries: a meta-analytic review. *Psychological Bulletin*, *136*(2), 151.

Bartholow, B. D., & Anderson, C. A. (2002). Effects of violent video games on aggressive behavior: Potential sex differences. *Journal of Experimental Social Psychology*, *38*(3), 283–290.

Brown, J. (1999). Doom, Quake and mass murder. *Salon*. Retrieved from http://www.salon.com/1999/04/23/gamers/

Dietz, T. L. (1998). An examination of violence and gender role portrayals in video games: Implications for gender socialization and aggressive behavior. *Sex Roles*, *38*(5–6), 425–442.

Dill, K. E., Gentile, D. A., Richter, W. A., & Dill, J. C. (2005). Violence, sex, race, and age in popular video Games: A content analysis.

Ferguson, C. J., & Kilburn, J. (2009). The public health risks of media violence: A meta-analytic review. *Journal of Pediatrics*, *154*, 759–763.

Ferguson, C. J. (2007a). Evidence for publication bias in video game violence effects literature: A meta-analytic review. *Aggression and Violent Behavior*, *12*, 470–482.

Ferguson, C. (2013). Adam Lanza's motive a mystery in Sandy Hook killings. *CNN*. http://edition.cnn.com/2013/11/27/opinion/ferguson-sandy-hook/

Ferguson, C. J. (2007a). The good, the bad and the ugly: A meta-analytic review of positive and negative effects of violent video games. *Psychiatric Quarterly*, *78*(4), 309–316.

Ferguson, C. J., Rueda, S. M., Cruz, A. M., Ferguson, D. E., Fritz, S., & Smith, S. M. (2008). Violent video games and aggression causal relationship or byproduct of family violence and intrinsic violence motivation? *Criminal Justice and Behavior*, *35*(3), 311–332.

Funk, J. B., Baldacci, H. B., Pasold, T., & Baumgardner, J. (2004). Violence exposure in real-life, video games, television, movies, and the internet: is there desensitization? *Journal of Adolescence, 27*(1), 23–39.

Hartmann, T., Krakowiak, K. M., & Tsay-Vogel, M. (2014). How violent video games communicate violence: A literature review and content analysis of moral disengagement factors. *Communication Monographs, 81*(3), 310–332.

Ivory, J. D., & Kalyanaraman, S. (2007). The effects of technological advancement and violent content in video games on players' feelings of presence, involvement, physiological arousal, and aggression. *Journal of Communication, 57*(3), 532–555.

Ivory, J. D., Williams, D., Martins, N., & Consalvo, M. (2009). Good clean fun? A content analysis of profanity in video games and its prevalence across game systems and ratings. *CyberPsychology & Behavior, 12*(4), 457–460.

MCV (2010). Violent Video Game Ban Passes In Switzerland. *Huffingtonpost.com.* http://www.huffingtonpost.com/2010/03/22/violent-video-game-ban-pa_n_507943.html

Pidd, H. (2012). Anders Breivik 'trained' for shooting attacks by playing *Call of Duty. The Guardian.* http://www.theguardian.com/world/2012/apr/19/anders-breivik-call-of-duty

Reed, A. (2014). 18 games banned across the world, and why they got the ax. *Gamesradar.com.* http://www.gamesradar.com/top-18-banned-video-games/

Rogers, R. (in press). The harm of video games: The ethics behind regulating minors' access to violent video games in light of the supreme court ruling. In. P. Booth and A. Davisson (Eds.), *Controversies in media ethics.* Bloomsbury

Rogers, R. (2012). Video game design and acceptance of hate speech in online gaming. In. R. A. Lind (Ed.), *Race/gender/class/media.* New York: Pearson.

Roskos-Ewoldsen, D. R., Roskos-Ewoldsen, B., & Carpentier, F. R. D. (2002). Media priming: A synthesis. *Media effects: Advances in theory and research, 2,* 97–120.

Scott, D. (1995). The effect of video games on feelings of aggression. *The Journal of Psychology, 129*(2), 121–132.

Sherry, J. L. (2001). The effects of violent video games on aggression. *Human Communication Research, 27*(3), 409–431.

Smith, S. L., Lachlan, K., & Tamborini, R. (2003). Popular video games: Quantifying the presentation of violence and its context. *Journal of Broadcasting & Electronic Media, 47*(1), 58–76.

Sweeting, P. (2005). Hot coffee burns. *VideoBusiness.* 25(30), 14.

Thompson, K. M., & Haninger, K. (2001). Violence in E-rated video games. *JAMA, 286*(5), 591–598.

Williams, D. (2003). The video game lightning rod. *Information Communication & Society, 6*(4), 523–550.

Yenigun, S. (2013). Video game violence: Why do we like it, and what's it doing to us? *NPR.* http://www.npr.org/2013/02/11/171698919/video-game-violence-why-do-we-like-it-and-whats-it-doing-to-us

Zillmann, D. (1971). Excitation transfer in communication-mediated aggressive behavior. *Journal of Experimental Social Psychology, 7*(4), 419–434.

Chapter Eight

Harassment

Online environments allow hate groups to organize and disseminate harassing messages as well as bullies to victimize others in unprecedented ways (Gerstenfeld, Grant, & Chiang, 2003; Hinduja & Patchin, 2014). Social media sites such as Facebook and YouTube feature user-generated content such as "Kill a Jew Day," "Kill a Beaner Day," an "Execute the Gays Page," and a "Murder Muslim Scum Page" (Citron & Norton, 2011). Meanwhile, Hinduja and Patchin (2014) detail several anecdotes of bullying through new media in their work. More specific to video games, some hate-based content has been developed. In the video game *Ethnic Cleansing*, the players' objective is to save the white "master race" by killing African Americans, Jews, and Hispanic Americans noted to be "subhuman" (Saunders, 2004). Also, there is a video game called *Beat Up Anita Sarkeesian* based on the 2014 Gamergate controversy. For brief background on Gamergate, a female video game developer, Zoe Quinn, was accused of using her sexuality to garner positive reviews for her game from a video game website. One woman who stood up for Quinn, Anita Sarkeesian, became the target of threats and harassment. The game is described as follows:

> Anita Sarkeesian has not only scammed thousands of people out of over $160,000, but also uses the excuse that she is a woman to get away with whatever she damn well pleases. Any form of constructive criticism, even from fellow women, is either ignored or labeled to be sexist against her. She claims to want gender equality in video games, but in reality, she just wants to use the fact that she was born with a vagina to get free money and sympathy from everyone who crosses her path.

This description of the game is more an attack on Sarkeesian than on the game itself. In the game, players click a picture of Sakeesian to "beat" her.

With each click the image of Sarkessian receives a black eye, swollen lip, or bloodied nose. In this manner, the game may be interpreted as intimidation and harassment of Sarkeesian.

Beyond the content of video games that might be considered harassment, many games allow players to interact with one another via voice chat or text chat. This chat feature is a major social and strategic part of certain video game communities (Valentine, 2014; Warner & Raiter, 2005). However, many of these interactions are charged with hateful, aggressive, racist, sexist, and otherwise harassing content.

Harassment in the video game community can be understood in the context of bullying and cyberbullying. While there are nuanced definitions of bullying, the broadly accepted conceptualization considers bullying aggressive behavior in which one is exerting power over another (Chesney, Coyne, Logan, & Madden, 2009; Olweus, 1994). This power can be derived from social hierarchy or physical strength among other power dynamics. Broadly speaking, cyberbullying and harassment in online venues can take a variety of shapes; threatening or embarrassing others via text, email, or social media are all considered cyberbullying (David-Ferdon & Hertz, 2007). Hinduja and Patchin (2014) say that cyberbullying is deliberate, repeated, harmful behavior done via electronic devices. The issue of online harassment and cyberbullying has grown to the extent that is has attracted the attention of the Centers for Disease Control, but the CDC's definition is more broad: electronic aggression (Centers for Disease Control, 2015).

Intuitively, anonymity might explain much of the harassment and bullying found in video games. Literature indicates that people say and do things in online environments that they would not do in person (Chesney, 2005; O'Sullivan & Flanagin, 2003). Deindividuation, or the loss of self-awareness, suggests that people lower their inhibitions when they no longer feel like individuals because they do not feel accountable for their actions (Festinger, Pepitone, & Newcomb, 1952). Evidence of this phenomenon shows that larger group size can decrease self-awareness (Diener, Lusk, DeFour, & Flax, 1980). Similarly, trick-or-treating children were more likely to steal candy when they were anonymous and when they were in a group (Diener, Fraser, Beaman, & Kelem, 1976). In video game environments, players are often anonymous as they are concealed behind a username and avatar. In this instance, the low fidelity of self-presentation allows for deindividuation. The avatar often cannot be identified as a specific person in the physical world. This feeling is exacerbated by the massive popularity of video games such that there are large groups playing games. Online gamers are literally one of millions (Deleon, 2010; Raby, 2011). A meta-analysis of deindividuation studies showed that people tend to alter their behaviors based on specific situations (Postmes & Spears, 1998). In that vein, online games may present unique scenarios that encourage deindividuation because players are anonymous and shielded from relevant social norms (Chesney et. al., 2009). Indeed, anonymous gaming predicts more breaches of the code of conduct (Chen & Wu, 2013).

This is certainly a viable explanation for harassment in online environments broadly; however, are there aspects of video games that might uniquely influence harassment behaviors? To explore this, qualitative interviews with online gamers were performed via headset (Rogers, 2012a). That is, interviews were conducted in a natural online gaming setting. The interviews revealed that anonymity played a major role in harassment behaviors such that players could easily escape from situations and there were minimal consequences for behaving in this manner. One participant said, "The anonymity of it brings out the worst in people" and other sentiments argued that the inability to link commenters with their accounts encouraged harassment behaviors. However, perhaps more interestingly, these interviews suggested that when video games encouraged competition that prompted more harassment. For example, interviewees stated:

- Harassment is "a way to just piss another person off and get them distracted thinking about the comment instead of the game."
- "In death matches (head-to-head, statistic driven game types) you're bound to hear that stuff."
- "Like in a sporting event, teams talk trash to each other."
- "It's always in-game when people are adrenaline packed and screaming random crap."

In short, harassment in competitive video games is not only expected but is believed to give the harasser an advantage over his or her victim. This is important because many video games feature at least some form of competition. Some games place players directly into competition with one another, like sports games such as *FIFA* and *Madden*. Or games ask players to kill one another as in *Halo* or *Counter-Strike*. Or games ask players to form a team to beat another team as in *League of Legends*. Meanwhile, other video games that are primarily cooperative—competitive point accrual notwithstanding—offer deathmatch modes in which players compete with one another. Even when video games do not pit players directly against one another, the games can still foster competition. Consider a video game like *Pac-Man*. Players are trying to eat dots, not each other. But the video game displays high scores fostering competition against one another. Consequently, if the rules of a video game promote competitive play, they are likely contributing to harassment behaviors. Likewise, if feedback is presented as a comparison to other players, this will likely lead to competition which will then lead to more harassment behaviors.

Similarly, when players felt that interaction with other players was mediated, the interaction felt less "real" (Rogers, 2012a). When it felt less real, harassment was described as more acceptable and more commonplace. When loading screens and other elements broke up a conversation and called attention to mediation, the interaction felt less real, and thus harassment behaviors became more acceptable. According to these responses, when the interaction did not feel like a face-to-face conversation the more likely harassment behaviors would manifest. Consider these sample quotes about harassment in video games:

- "In games you are only a voice so how can you be prejudiced?"
- "Who do you really meet? I had a conversation with this guy in a chat room last night but I didn't actually meet them."
- "It can be not directed toward anybody. It can go in one ear and out the other."
- "I just don't think this is a venue that I want to have anything like making real friends or talking to people about serious things. This is a venue for entertainment and nothing more to me."

This finding suggests that interface design elements can have a bearing on harassment. If a loading screen is placed at an inopportune time or if players can drop in and drop out of chat rooms easily, then harassing behaviors might be common. Within the context of feedback, this suggests that when feedback loops are interrupted, players will engage in more harassment. This likely reflects how people are accustomed to certain feedback loops when interacting with others. When this familiar feedback loop is interrupted then the interactions do not feel real. A more consistent feedback loop for player-to-player communication might alter harassment behaviors.

While this qualitative data is informative, an experiment tested how competition and mediated interactions impact acceptance of harassment behaviors (Rogers, 2012b). In this experiment, video game players rated their approval of things happening (different types of comments, unsportsmanlike play, cheating, etc.) in a pre-taped game session. Participants either watched a more competitive game mode in which the objective was to eliminate the opponent to score points or a more cooperative game in which the objective was to control portions of the map in order to gain points. Segments of the game were also highly mediated or lowly mediated such that natural dialogue was interrupted at certain points and not at others. The results showed that those viewing the competitive game mode were more accepting of the use of harassing phrases in the game than those watching the cooperative game mode. Likewise, during moments that were perceived to be highly mediated, participants were more accepting of harassing terms than during moments that were perceived to be less mediated. Again, this demonstrates that design choices in video games, specifically related to rules and feedback, can alter the way in which people are interacting.

Notably, the harassment in this experiment was in the form of terms like "faggot" or "bitch." As such, video games might sometimes encourage a patriarchal hierarchy such that masculine traits, like competition, are valued and harassment that makes a player seem less masculine is acceptable. Women tend to be targets for harassment in the video game community (Yee, 2008). Indeed, women have not been made to feel welcome in the video game community since the days of video game arcades in the 1980s (Wilder, Mackie, & Cooper, 1985). Arcades were male-dominated and women were viewed as spectators while the men played. In a contemporary setting, Yee (2008) explored why women did not feel welcome in the video game community. Yee found that women experienced harassment in several forms. Some were content-based but others were based on the video game community:

- Female players are frequently questioned if they are just pretending to be female.
- Female players are accused of playing only because a male in their lives wants them to, like a boyfriend or husband.
- There are frequent suggestions that women could not be intrinsically motivated to play a game. Female players only use games for ulterior motives, such as garnering attention from a community of men.
- Female players are often subjected to unsolicited sexual advances while playing online video games. Women are objects for the consumption and pleasure of men in this community.

Conversely, a survey on harassment revealed that women who played online games encountered no more harassment than those who use other new media platforms (Norris, 2004). Similarly, women who played video games were not any more accepting of sexual violence toward women nor were they more masculine than women who did not play video games. This indicates that the concerns about harassment and misogyny in the video game community might be overstated. Or more likely, Norris (2004) extrapolates from these findings that perhaps women who experience harassment in video games do not continue playing or women were only reporting harassment in regard to extreme instances.

Often, harassment behaviors in video games might be considered griefing (Warner & Raiter, 2005), although griefing does tend to have a broader definition. Griefing has been described as harassment related to discrimination, sexual harassment, and using distracting or improper communication in video games (Kolo & Baur, 2004). Another definition of griefing is "intentional harassment of other players" by breaking game rules or using unintended styles of play in order to upset other players (Warner & Raiter, 2005, p. 45). Another definition argues that griefing is "purposefully engaging in activities to disrupt the gaming experience of other players" (Mulligan & Patrovsky, 2003, p. 250). Griefing can include but goes beyond acts of cheating (Chesney et. al., 2009).

In one popular online game, *World of Warcraft*, players can impede the progress of others by exploiting game mechanics. Warner and Raiter (2005) detail a "Corrupted Blood" spell that allowed players who had "stored" this disease to easily and quickly wipe out lower level players with the disease. Given that this was not the game designers' intended purpose of the spell, the game designers altered the game rules after realizing how it had been used to harass certain players. Warner and Raiter (2005) detail another manner in which grieifing occurs in *World of Warcraft*: spawn camping. This refers to a player waiting in a certain area for a second player to respawn, or come back to life, only to kill that second player again and again. Consequently, the weaker player is stuck in a situation where he or she is killed instantly or nearly instantly each time he or she spawns. This tactic is not limited to *World of Warcraft* and can be seen in other games as well. It is likely that players often spawn camp because it is allowed by the rules and the feedback system rewards the behavior and thereby encourages it.

In a more child-friendly online game, *Toon Town*, one might expect that griefing would be uncommon. However, players find unique ways to grief one another even when the game rules attempt to discourage it (Warner & Raiter, 2005). In the case of *Toon Town*, players are only allowed to speak with each other if both players consent to open lines of communication. Without consent, however, players can use shorter, predetermined emotes. A game experience can be ruined by one player following another and repeatedly using an emote (Warner & Raiter, 2005). On a fundamental level, the feedback of pressing a button and seeing instant impact on the screen is satisfying. On a deeper level, players are rearticulating the rules and pushing the latitude that the rules afford.

In their highly detailed exploration of griefing in *Second Life*, Chesney et al., (2009) state that griefing is any behavior deemed unacceptable by that game's community. As an aside, this book does not necessarily classify *Second Life* as a video game. Instead, it is more accurately described as a virtual world. Accordingly, Chesney et al. (2009) note that the nature of *Second Life* makes griefing a bit different than griefing in other online venues. Regardless, their discussion of griefing remains germane. Chesney et al. (2009) argue that griefing often presents no physical threat and the griefer and the griefee rarely know one another. Further, they suggest that griefing is easily avoided at the cost of fully enjoying what a particular game has to offer. This means that someone can avoid a griefer by avoiding certain aspects of a game.

According to the *Second Life* policies, the following acts are prohibited and thus can be construed as griefing: intolerance, harassment, assault, disclosure, indecency, and disturbing the peace. Both the Playstation Network's and Xbox Live's online gaming policies explicitly forbid harassment. Despite these policies, such behaviors appear to be common. Nearly all of a sample of *Second Life* users had experienced griefing with over a third suggesting that it happened frequently (Coyne, Chesney, Logan, & Madden, 2009). Chesney et al.'s (2009) observations included but were not limited to: verbal harassment, acts of violence, giving away others' personal information, swearing, and repetition of sights/sounds. In their focus groups they discovered that griefing was common yet unacceptable. However, some thought griefing was harmless in spite of significant impacts it can have. Players are able to grief because the rules are not enforced effectively. The policies are clear but the ramifications are not. This highlights the interconnected nature of rules and feedback. What is in place is a rule without effective feedback. This results in the goal of reduced harassment not being met. Thus, griefing, in certain contexts, occupies a space where some view it as culturally and socially relevant (Bakioglu, 2009).

From a legal perspective, video games in the United States are afforded a large degree of protection under the First Amendment. Indeed, harassment in video games would have to cause an immediate breach of the peace in order for regulation to be justified. As a result, the rules of the companies that host and create these games are the most viable avenue for reducing harassment (Citron & Norton, 2011). On the other hand, some online gaming communities have attempted to police themselves independently of the content producers. In one game, *Tapu*, the community voted on new rules governing harassment for the community (Nakamura, 1995). The aim was to punish those who engaged in harassing practices but the vote failed. Many felt that identity was obscured in this online venue and thus one could easily escape harassment. The community, perhaps unknowingly, was referring to the notion of transformed social interaction (TSI; Bailenson, Beall, Loomis, Blascovich, & Turk, 2004). TSI essentially describes the ability to alter social situations in virtual environments that cannot be altered in the physical world—a concept central to understanding self-presentation in video games (Yee, Bailenson, & Ducheneaut, 2009). For example, a white, heterosexual, male may be allowed to experience a video game as a black, homosexual, female. Thus, virtual environments allow for self-presentation that muddles what might be considered harassment inside and outside of the game space. In essence, a player can be placed into the role of a minority within the game space. This could be used to obscure the player's real identity or, perhaps more interestingly, to allow the player to come as close as he or she can to taking the perspective of someone with a different demographic makeup. If the player's demographics and the avatar's demographics are incongruent then how should harassment directed at one of those demographics be interpreted? Where does the avatar begin and where does the player end? These questions are important to consider and merit further exploration.

Overall, the way a game is designed dictates how people interact in the game. The rules and feedback in particular can be used to enforce or discourage harassment while differences in self-presentation allow players to experience multiple perspectives in relation to harassment and also raise important questions about the nature of harassment in video games.

REFERENCES

Bailenson, J. N., Beall, A. C., Loomis, J., Blascovich, J., & Turk, M. (2004). Transformed social interaction: Decoupling representation from behavior and form in collaborative virtual environments. *PRESENCE: Teleoperators and Virtual Environments, 13*(4), 428–441.

Bakioglu, B. S. (2009). Spectacular interventions of second life: Goon culture, griefing, and disruption in virtual spaces. *Journal for Virtual Worlds Research, 1*(3).

Centers for Disease Control (2015). Electronic aggression. *CDC.gov*. http://www.cdc.gov/ViolencePrevention/youthviolence/electronicaggression/index.html

Chen, V. H. H., & Wu, Y. (2013). Group identification as a mediator of the effect of players' anonymity on cheating in online games. *Behaviour & Information Technology* (ahead-of-print), 1–10.

Chesney, T. (2005) Online self disclosure in diaries and its implications for knowledge managers. UKAIS Conference, 22–24 March, Northumbria University, Newcastle, UK.

Chesney, T., Coyne, I., Logan, B., & Madden, N. (2009). Griefing in virtual worlds: causes, casualties and coping strategies. *Information Systems Journal, 19*(6), 525–548.

Citron, D. K., & Norton, H. (2011). Intermediaries and hate speech: Fostering digital citizenship for our information age. *Boston University Law Review, 91*, 1435.

Coyne, I., Chesney, T., Logan, B., & Madden, N. (2009). Griefing in a virtual community. *Zeitschrift für Psychologie/Journal of Psychology, 217*(4), 214–221.

David-Ferdon, C., & Hertz, M. F. (2007). Electronic media, violence, and adolescents: An emerging public health problem. *Journal of Adolescent Health, 41*(6), S1–S5.

Deleon, N. (2010). Microsoft: Only 50 percent of Xbox Live users pay for gold subscription. *Techcrunch.com*. http://techcrunch.com/2010/12/02/microsoft-only-50-percent-of-xbox-live-users-pay-for-gold-subscription/

Diener, E., Lusk, R., DeFour, D., & Flax, R. (1980). Deindividuation: Effects of group size, density, number of observers, and group member similarity on self-consciousness and disinhibited behavior. *Journal of Personality and Social Psychology, 39*(3), 449.

Diener, E., Fraser, S. C., Beaman, A. L., & Kelem, R. T. (1976). Effects of deindividuation variables on stealing among Halloween trick-or-treaters. *Journal of Personality and Social Psychology, 33*(2), 178.

Dyer, R., Green, R., Pitts, M., & Millward, G. (1995). What's the flaming problem? Or computer mediated communication-deindividuating or disinhibiting?. In M. A. R. Kirby, A. J. Dix & J. E. Finlay (Eds.) *People and Computers X* (pp. 289–302). Cambridge: Cambridge University Press.

Festinger, L., Pepitone, A., & Newcomb, T. (1952). Some consequences of deindividuation in a group. *Journal of Abnormal and Social Psychology, 47*, 382–389.

Gerstenfeld, P. B., Grant, D. R., & Chiang, C. P. (2003). Hate online: A content analysis of extremist Internet sites. *Analyses of Social Issues and Public Policy, 3*(1), 29–44.

Griffiths, M. D., Davies, M. N., & Chappell, D. (2003). Breaking the stereotype: The case of online gaming. *CyberPsychology & Behavior, 6*(1), 81–91.

Hinduja, S., & Patchin, J. W. (2014). *Bullying beyond the schoolyard: Preventing and responding to cyberbullying*. Thousand Oaks, CA: Corwin Press.

Kolo, C., & Baur, T. (2004). Living a virtual life: Social dynamics of online gaming. *Game Studies*, *4*(1), 1–31.

Mulligan, J., & Patrovsky, B. (2003). *Developing online games: An insider's guide*. Indianapolis, IN: New Riders.

Nakamura, L. (1995). Race in/for cyberspace: Identity tourism and racial passing on the Internet. *Works and Days*, *25*(26), 13.

Norris, K. O. (2004). Gender stereotypes, aggression, and computer games: an online survey of women. *Cyberpsychology & Behavior*, *7*(6), 714–727.

Olweus, D. (1994). *Bullying at school* (pp. 97–130). Springer US.

O'Sullivan, P. B., & Flanagin, A. J. (2003). Reconceptualizing 'flaming'and other problematic messages. *New Media & Society*, *5*(1), 69–94.

Postmes, T., & Spears, R. (1998). Deindividuation and antinormative behavior: A meta-analysis. *Psychological Bulletin*, *123*(3), 238.

Raby, M. (2011). PSN has twice as many users as Xbox Live. *Gamesradar.com*. http://www.gamesradar.com/psn-has-twice-as-many-users-as-xbox-live/

Rogers, R. (2012a). The virtual locker room: Hate speech and online gaming. *Journal of New Media and Culture*, *8*(1).

Rogers, R. (2012b). Video game design and acceptance of hate speech in online gaming. In. R. A. Lind (Ed.), *Race/gender/class/media*. New York: Pearson.

Saunders, K. W. (2004). The need for a two (or more) tiered First Amendment to provide for the protection of children. *Chicago-Kent Law Review*, *79*, 257–277.

Valentine, J. (2014). The lack of in-game communication in Destiny is troubling. *Gamezone.com*. http://www.gamezone.com/news/the-lack-of-in-game-communication-in-destiny-is-troubling

Warner, D. E., & Raiter, M. (2005). Social context in massively-multiplayer online games (MMOGs): Ethical questions in shared space. *International Review of Information Ethics*, *4*(7).

Wilder, G., Mackie, D., & Cooper, J. (1985). Gender and computers: Two surveys of computer-related attitudes. *Sex Roles*, *13*(3), 215–228.

Yee, N. (2008). Maps of digital desires: Exploring the topography of gender and play in online games. In Y. B. Kafai, C. Heeter, J. Denner & J. Y. Sun (Eds.) *Beyond Barbie and Mortal Kombat: New perspectives on gender and gaming*, 83–96. Cambridge, MA: MIT Press.

Yee, N., Bailenson, J. N., & Ducheneaut, N. (2009). The Proteus effect: Implications of transformed digital self-representation on online and offline behavior. *Communication Research*, *36*, 285–312.

Chapter Nine

Diversity Issues

Coinciding with harassment of people from certain demographics, video game content tends to not be diverse. Specifically, video games tend to feature white, male protagonists while most other demographics are under-represented. A study by Williams, Martins, Consalvo, and Ivory (2009) examined the top 150 video games for portrayals of gender and race. They found that men were represented 85 percent of the time while women were only represented 15 percent of the time. This runs in contrast to a nearly 50/50 split in the actual population. The authors note that this difference is exaggerated when considering the main character of the game as opposed to any character in the game.

The racial breakdown of video game characters compared to the actual population is similarly disparate:

- Whites are overrepresented in video games by nearly 7 percent.
- Asians are overrepresented in video games by nearly 26 percent.
- Blacks are underrepresented in video games by nearly 13 percent.
- Hispanics are underrepresented in video games by 78 percent.
- Native Americans are underrepresented in video games by 90 percent.

Again, these contrasts are starker when considering the video game's protagonist as opposed to all characters in the game. Since the protagonist is white 85 percent of the time in video games, this leaves very few protagonists spread across the other demographics.

In the rare occasions that characters other than white males are portrayed, they are portrayed stereotypically (Burgess, Dill, Stermer, Burgess, & Brown, 2011). Stereotypes are beliefs about certain types of people designed to lower cognitive burden (Fiske, 1998). In other words, stereotypes are generalizations about groups of people that help organize and simplify cognitions. However, stereotypes can be inaccurate, overbroad, or even damaging (Chalabaev, Sarrazin, Fontayne, Boiché, & Clément-Guillotin, 2013; Steele & Aronson, 1995). All types of video games have relied on stereotypes—high quality games, poor quality games, old games, new games, commercial games, and educational games. Many games have relied on gender stereotypes:

- In *Duke Nukem Forever* (2011) the player assumes the role of the hyper-macho Duke. He has twin girlfriends ready to please him with sexual favors and by promising that they will lose weight. The game also features the execution of naked, pregnant women, oozing phalluses, and breasts on the walls that bounce when slapped (Stevens, 2013). The game also features a "Catch the Babe" mode where players capture women to score points (Billington, 2014). The women become upset when captured and the player slaps the women to calm them down.
- *Bayonetta* (2010): A critically acclaimed game in which the protagonist is a dominatrix clad in leather designed to fulfill male fantasy (Stevens, 2013). In fact, sex was one of the developer's key selling points of the game (Billington, 2014).
- *Dead or Alive Paradise* (2010): In this spinoff series that was panned by critics, players go to an island resort to ogle and befriend busty women in bikinis. Players can also buy new outfits for the women (Stevens, 2013). The game designer said in an interview that if players masturbated to the game, it would be considered a success (Elise, 2014).
- *Street Fighter 2* (1991) features only one female character. Game designers considered making her health bar shorter than the other characters' simply because she was a woman.
- The role-playing game, *Dragon Quest VIII* (2005) features a female character with oversized, bouncing breasts. The character's equipment is also highly sexualized. Players can choose to put the woman into a bunny outfit, a bikini, or a bustier. Lastly, the character can distract enemies by shaking her bottom at them (Stevens, 2013).
- *Tomb Raider* (series): The main character, Lara Croft, has become a gaming icon with an unrealistic hourglass figure. Despite her role as a heroine and a potentially positive role model, her figure has received the most attention (Stevens, 2013). In fact, rumors of "naked codes" emerged surrounding the character such that a player could enter a complex string of inputs to see the character nude (Walker, 2007).
- *League of Legends* (2009): A game popular for competitive gamers, features a scantily clad huntress who reminds players that it is "mating season" (Stevens, 2013).

- *Metroid Other M* (2010) turned one of the most beloved female video game characters, Samus Aran, into a weak, submissive woman (Stevens, 2013). In the original *Metroid* (1986), the end of the game revealed Samus as a woman. This was one of the most iconic moments for women in video games (Ashcraft, 2010), so the reduction of Samus to a stereotype was distressing for fans.
- *God of War III* (2010) allows the player to put the main character, a man, into orgies with multiple women, sometimes with a female audience (Elise, 2014).
- In *Catherine* (2011) the protagonist must choose between two female stereotypes, a controlling girlfriend and a femme fatale (Elise, 2014).
- *Lollipop Chainsaw* (2012) features a sexualized cheerleader battling zombies who poses seductively for the player (Billington, 2014).

In these video games, women are presented stereotypically as highly sexualized objects, irritating, and stupid. These sexualized representations are especially evident when examining breast physics. Breast physics in video refers to the animation of a female video game character's breasts in order for the characters to seem more realistic or more sexually appealing (Giantbomb.com, 2014). A recent study found that discourse related to breast physics in video games indicates that breasts are to be consumed in the masculine space of video games (Rogers & Liebler, 2015). Breast physics provide the player feedback in the form of swinging breasts. Players are allowed to gratify their desires by moving the character in certain ways which may move the female figure in an appealing manner. Further, players' self-presentation is a factor to consider. If the player assumes the role of the female character, he or she assumes control over that character. This power dynamic allows players to further their objectification of the characters as they can control exactly what the character does and how the character looks. Moreover, if a player assumes the role of a male in a game, the player is placed in the shoes of a masculine character often aroused by the female characters surrounding them.

While there are gender stereotypes in video games, there are also racial stereotypes:

- *Street Fighter 2* is noted for some racially problematic content (Demby, 2014; Leone, 2014). Some in the black community were upset that a cut scene early in the game featured a white man knocking out a black man in front of a crowd of cheering white people. Beyond that, the cast of characters in the game relies on cultural stereotypes. E. Honda is a sumo wrestler who fights in a bathhouse. Dhalsim is an Indian man who fights with yoga style in front of elephants. Zangief is a burly, hairy Russian. Guile is a blond American warhawk.

- Another classic, *Mike Tyson's Punch-Out!!!* features stereotypes from around the world (Demby, 2014). Don Flamenco is an effeminate Spaniard. Great Tiger is a turban-wearing Indian. Von Kaiser is a militant German.
- Even one of the most famous classic video games, *Super Mario Brothers* relies on Italian stereotypes (Demby, 2014; Hester, 2012) and one of the first enemies Mario encounters is a "goomba," a term that can be derogatory toward Italians.
- *Scribblenauts*, a game that can be educational, allows players to bring objects and people into the game by writing different words. For example, typing in "dog" would make a dog appear in the game. Typing in the word "Sambo" generates a watermelon (Raith, 2012). "Sambo" is a slur toward blacks and the watermelon is a reference to the stereotype that blacks consume a lot of watermelon.
- Similar to *Street Fighter 2* and *Punch Out!!!*, *Freaky Flyers* (Hester, 2012; Raith, 2012) also used racial stereotypes. Characters in the game include a Middle Eastern oil tycoon who flies on a magic carpet and a buck-toothed Japanese kamikaze pilot named Sammy Wasabi.
- An educational video game, *Spanish For Everyone*, portrays Mexicans through a variety of stereotypes like drug cartel members, thieves, and seductresses (Hester, 2012; Raith, 2012).
- *Homie Rollerz*, a game based off of the popular toys, presents Hispanics as gang members (Raith, 2012). Players can even have their characters use a big burrito with wheels as a vehicle.
- In *Grand Theft Auto San Andreas*, players can compete in a "kill the cholos" mission in which the player kills Mexican gang members (Hester, 2012). "Cholo" is a slur toward Mexican-Americans.
- *Border Patrol 2002* encourages the player to shoot Mexicans crossing the U.S. border (Hester, 2012).
- In *Resident Evil 5* (2009) players must contain an outbreak of disease in Africa partly mirroring real-life events. Players use a white character to kill legions of infected black locals (Sargent, 2012).
- In *Diablo* 3, only one playable character is black. He has a thick accent and is a witch doctor (Sargent, 2012).
- *Call of Juarez: The Cartel*, a game about Mexican drug wars, relies on racial stereotypes for both the story and game play (Sargent, 2012). In one mission, players are rewarded for killing black characters.

While some of these portrayals may seem trivial and others may seem patently offensive, it is important to consider how these portrayals impact audience perceptions. The impact of stereotypes, even positive stereotypes, is tangible and supported by empirical evidence.

On a fundamental level, underrepresentation and stereotypical representations impact the consumption of media. In one study, black and white participants were asked to browse news websites (Knobloch-Westerwick, Appiah, & Alter, 2008). White participants showed no preference based on the race of the person in the news story. However, black participants were much more likely to read a news story featuring a black person. Indeed, people may consume or avoid media in order to gratify their social identities (Abrams & Giles, 2007). In other words, race and gender can determine what content people consume when that content presents certain demographics. For example, a black male in his 40s living in California may not watch an episode of *Girls*, a show about white women in their mid-20s living in New York City, because he does not see himself in the content. The financial repercussions of this are clear: by excluding certain demographics from video games, game producers limit the appeal of that game. Thus, when consumers see the self presented in content, or at least a closer approximation of the self, he or she will be more likely to consume that content. Notably, findings using this line of reasoning are not always consistent (Coleman, 2011) and should be interpreted as such.

Furthermore, underrepresentation and misrepresentation of certain demographics can give players misinformed perceptions. According to cultivation theory, people who consume a large amount of media perceive the world to reflect that media (Gerbner, Gross, Morgan, & Signorielli, 1986). An example used to illustrate this: A person who watches a lot of violent television perceives the world to be more violent than it actually is. In the context of demographic portrayals in video games, people who play a lot of video games will perceive the world to have unrealistic demographics or that misrepresentations of race and gender found in video games can be found in the physical world.

For an example of how stereotypical portrayals impact audience members, participants viewed racial stereotypes of African American women (mammy, an overweight maternal figure, or jezebel, a woman with loose morals) in media, then sat in on mock employment interviews (Brown Givens & Monahan, 2005). African American job candidates were more readily associated with traits related to negative stereotypes than with traits related to positive stereotypes. In another study, Latino high school students who watched a lot of television reported lower self-esteem than those who watched less television (Rivadeneyra, Ward, & Gordon, 2007). The suggestion is that the students become accustomed to underrepresentation or stereotypical presentation of Latinos and other minorities on television and thus think worse of themselves. Importantly, low self-esteem is connected to negative psychological effects (Sowislo & Orth, 2013).

In a follow-up study, the researchers showed a similar pattern with other minority groups such that people who viewed television programs that reinforced positive Asian American stereotypes had more positive attitudes toward Asian Americans and more negative attitudes toward African Americans, such that Asians are, stereotypically, a more likeable minority (Dalisay & Tan, 2009; Ramasubramanian, 2011). Similarly, in an experiment, a suspect in a crime story was either black or white (Dixon, 2006). People who watched a lot of television news were more likely to think that a black suspect was guilty and culpable for the crime as opposed to a white suspect. This was due to the common representation of black males as criminals on television. These presentations can even impact content producers such that journalists' ethical reasoning was higher when the subject of a story was white than when the subject was black (Coleman, 2003). In each of these cases, the argument is that media representations of race and stereotypes impact how people act and think at a later date about people from that group.

While these articles tend to focus on stereotypical portrayals on television, these findings can be extrapolated beyond television (Oliver, 2003). That is, stereotypical portrayals in video games and other media can impact how players view certain groups of people as well. When boys and girls prefer stereotypical content broadly, it predicts stereotypical masculine and feminine traits in those boys and girls (Aubrey & Harrison, 2004). Those who prefer music genres that stereotype women, tend to feel more aggressive toward women and feel that women are not trustworthy (Rubin, West, & Mitchell, 2001). Women who view movies that portray young women with negative stereotypes tend to fulfill those roles in their own lives (Behm-Morawitz & Mastro, 2008). When using a male or female character in a video game, players fulfill roles more stereotypical of the character's gender (Yang, Huesmann, & Bushman, 2014). In terms of race, playing anti-terrorism video games with portrayals of Arabs can increase anti-Arab attitudes (Saleem & Anderson, 2013). Some of these examples are not causal but the relationship between consuming stereotypical content and attitudes/behaviors toward that group has been demonstrated. Perhaps most importantly, the use of stereotypes can lead to stigmatization and discrimination (Link & Phelan, 2001) and video games may be contributing to this.

This book takes the position that the implementation of rules and feedback in video games has facilitated the presentation of stereotypes. Good video game rules must be easy to understand (Juul, 2011). Stereotypes, like rules, are designed to be easily understood (Fiske, 1998). If rules are too complex then a game becomes too cumbersome. Likewise, thinking about and interacting with each and every person creates a cognitive burden. Thus, for purposes of clarity and ease of understanding, games might use simplified mechanisms and representations. For example, in one game, the red team may try to kill the blue team. In a modern iteration of this game that uses more graphical fidelity and narrative elements, the counter-terrorist unit might fight against the terrorists. The counter-terrorists will look a certain way and the terrorists will look another way. These presentations are based on general beliefs about these groups, not specifics of the individuals. In fact, if each character were presented uniquely it would be difficult to identify which character was on which team. In that fashion, game play would be impeded and become more difficult to understand. Similarly, for a game to provide an effective feedback system it must be understood easily and thus presentations become deliberately rudimentary and broad. If a feedback system is not clearly communicated, it is ineffective, so presenting clear information quickly becomes paramount. Thus, stereotypes in games might actually provide more clear rules and feedback. Even so, more thoughtful portrayals could be used to curb some of the negative effects of stereotypical content. The remainder of this chapter will focus on portrayals of sex in video games.

Sex

Media content often portrays sex as exciting, fun, important, and consequence-free (Brown, Steele, & Walsh-Childers, 2001; Huston, Wartella, & Donnerstein, 1998; Strasburger, 2012). Moreover, presenting sex in media is a common practice because it is highly profitable (Bryant & Oliver, 2009) and some video games have adopted this business model. As video games advance in terms of photorealism and narrative complexity, they can portray sexual content with higher graphical fidelity and allow for the development of physical relationships between characters.

As detailed previously, most commercial video games are rated by the ESRB. In video games rated Mature (M), intended for adult audiences, 36 percent contained sexual content, while 17 percent contained depictions of prostitution (Thompson, Tepichin, & Haninger, 2006). In Teen (T) rated video games, intended for teenage audiences, 27 percent included sexual content (Haninger & Thompson, 2004). Sexual content in these contexts refers to provocative touching, moaning, and depictions of nudity but not provocative clothing. Even more noteworthy, sexual content was even found in children's video games rated E for Everyone (Thompson & Haninger, 2001). Broadly, it is accepted that sexual content is prevalent in video games (Stermer & Burkley, 2012).

Beyond in-game presentation of sex, the media surrounding video games contribute to a culture where women are treated as sexual objects to be used by the male players such that female characters and the female body are often put on display in sexually suggestive positions for the enjoyment of male video game players (Ivory, 2006). As mentioned, one video game developer noted for the sexy female characters in its games, Team Ninja, claimed that if players masturbate to their games, it is considered a "success" (Yin-Poole, 2010). There are even games that qualify as "porn games"—games intended to be used as pornography (Raith, 2012) —with some studios dedicated to developing them, not unlike the film industry (Campbell, 2013).

Notably, porn games, like pornographic movies, are not understood as mainstream video games; however, some mainstream video games feature strong sexual content. In order to develop an understanding of the nature of sex in commercial video games a list of mainstream video games that feature sexual content is detailed below:

- *Mass Effect* series: This video game features a complex story about space exploration and intergalactic politics. The player has the opportunity to pursue relationships and eventually have sexual intercourse with a variety of humans and aliens. Players can even pursue homosexual relationships in the game, a relatively unique feature for mainstream video games.
- *Fable* series: In these fantasy video games, players can engage in polygamy, extramarital affairs, and solicit prostitution. This sort of behavior can result in pregnancy as well as sexually transmitted disease. This is one of the few instances in which sex in video games is portrayed to have negative consequences analogous to the physical world.
- *God of War 3*: A game about mythical gods battling one another features nudity in a sex scene in which the player must push the right sequence of buttons in order to perform intercourse. Two topless women watch and admire the player's ability to pleasure the woman.
- *Grand Theft Auto* series: This game allows players to sleep with prostitutes or date and subsequently have sex with different women. Notoriously, one of the *Grand Theft Auto* games included a mod called Hot Coffee that made sex with a chosen in-game girlfriend into a minigame not unlike the *God of War* example described above.
- *Heavy Rain*: A game noted for its character development depicts a sex scene between two characters.
- *Far Cry 3*: The player controls a character that is transitioning from a privileged college student to a seasoned warrior. In order to become the warrior, the player has sex with a woman native to the game's island setting.
- *Leisure Suit Larry* series: This series focuses on the main character's comedic attempts to seduce women.
- *The Sims*: In this game players can develop relationships with other characters, which includes making out, trying for a baby, and "woohoo" which requires a bed or other item such as a shower or hot tub that enables "woohoo." Notably, "woohoo" can result in pregnancy.

These examples demonstrate that sexual content varies widely between games. Some video games require player participation in sex while some are completely passive. Other games allow the player to choose whether or not he or she will engage in intercourse while others offer the players no choice but to engage in sexual intercourse if they want to progress. Some video games portray sex as a romantic enterprise while others portray it as reward. Other games show sex in a realistic fashion while others portray it as a fantasy. In short, video games portray sex in ways similar to other media. However, these games provide a space where people can engage in sexual behaviors without risks found in the physical world like disease or unwanted pregnancy—virtual versions excluded. In this fashion, video game rules provide a safe place for players to representatively have sex. Meanwhile, the game's feedback pushes the player toward or away from sexual behaviors through rewards or punishment.

Despite the differences detailed above, each of the previous games featured consensual sex. However, there are also video games that depict rape and sexual violence.

- *Custer's Revenge*: Released in 1982, the object of the game is to navigate General Custer across the screen in order to rape a Native American woman.
- *Silent Hill 2*: One of the iconic monsters in this horror game is seen raping and subsequently killing another monster.
- *Rapelay*: Essentially a rape simulator, the player takes control of a man who stalks then rapes a woman and her daughters.
- *Battle Raper*: A fighting game that removes clothing from the female characters when they are attacked. In an additional play mode, players can molest the characters.

Various retailers like Amazon—not the government—have banned the sale of some of these games in the United States, but with so many digital distribution outlets, those who are motivated to play these video games could acquire them (Moore, 2009). This raises the question: What are the hazards of video games that allow or encourage players to perform sexual violence?

These portrayals of sex have garnered a fair amount of negative attention. Video games may have the connotation of children's toys but the content can be quite mature. For example, when one of the *Mass Effect* video games was released, it was criticized for targeting younger audiences despite its sexual content (MacCallum, 2008). The argument was made that young boys were given the opportunity to use women as sex objects, while a defender of the game argued that the reality—as constructed by the game—was much more nuanced. In *Dragon Age: Origins* a homosexual relationship between two male elves was implied, which some praised and others condemned (*The Week*, 2009).

Controversy aside, these portrayals could impact players' attitudes and behaviors related to sex (Harris & Barlett, 2009). On a fundamental level, exposure to sexual media content can alter a person's ability to positively interact with others (Villani, 2001) and leads to less progressive attitudes toward gender roles (Brown & L'Engle, 2009). Perhaps more importantly, exposure to sexual content in media encourages sexual activity at younger ages and thereby increases associated risks (Brown et al., 2006). Indeed, media portrayals of sex present a potential public health risk as they can contribute to the spread of sexually transmitted disease and an increase in youth pregnancy (Walsh & Gentile, 2001). In other words, the higher a youth's sexual media exposure, the more likely he or she is to have had sex and have sexual intentions (Pardun, L'Engle, & Brown, 2005; L'Engle, Brown, & Kenneavy, 2006). Notably, this pattern is found for pornographic content and non-pornographic sexual content (Brown & L'Engle, 2009). Similarly, one study suggested that those who were already sexually active were more likely to seek out media with sexual themes and those portrayals of sex encouraged further sexual activity (Bleakley, Hennessy, Fishbein, & Jordan, 2008), indicating a feedback loop of sexual behavior and consumption of sexual content. In any case, sexual media content becomes incorporated into the lives of adolescents and can have a bearing on that person's attitudes toward sex (Brown, 2000).

Evidence suggests that exposure to sexual content can diminish negative attitudes toward rape and increase aggression toward women (Allen, Emmers, Gebhardt, & Giery, 1995; Malamuth & Briere, 1986; Malamuth & Check, 1981). Violent sexual content can also desensitize audience members to sexual violence (Harris & Barlett, 2009; Mullin & Linz, 1995). Within a video game these concerns are likely exacerbated because the player may be the one performing the sex acts and the game might encourage or require behaviors to which certain audience members may have an aversion or susceptibility. A correlation between video game play and hostile sexism has been found (Fox & Potocki, 2015). Similarly, playing video games with sexist content is associated with sexist attitudes (Stermer & Burkley, 2015).

The argument that sexual content impacts users relies primarily on two theories described previously in this book: social cognitive theory (Bandura, 2001) and cultivation theory (Gerbner, Gross, Morgan, & Signorielli, 1986). Social cognitive theory suggests that people can learn behaviors from observing others perform the behaviors. For a sexual example, a video game might teach a player how to engage in sex acts as well as how to treat the individuals he or she has sex with. Furthermore, when a behavior in media content is rewarded, it is more likely to be modeled than when the behavior is punished. Thus, if sex is shown as pleasurable and fun without consequence, the behaviors will likely be modeled. Game rules and game feedback can thereby encourage or discourage sexual behavior and the corresponding attitudes. Notably, very few portrayals of sex in the media show the negative consequences or responsible models (Brown, 2002; Huston et al., 1998) so media typically encourage these behaviors. This appears to be consistent with video games as only two of the video games described above implemented any unintended consequences for engaging in sexual activity.

Cultivation theory, described above, argues that the more people spend time with media, the more they perceive the physical world to reflect the media world. For example, people who watch a lot of *Law & Order* would perceive that they are often in danger from criminals. Further, if sex is commonly shown to be fun and enjoyable without consequence in media, that is how those who consume a large degree of media will perceive it.

The pattern of sexual media consumption and sexual behaviors has been demonstrated with a variety of media (Klein et al., 1993) and a handful of studies have shown a similar pattern in video games. Sexual content in video games will likely only increase as content producers push the boundaries of the sexual content portrayed (Walsh & Gentile, 2001). For example, it will not be long before players can engage in fully immersive sexual content that uses haptic devices and virtual reality. The psychological impact of these advancements should be closely considered by researchers and practitioners alike.

REFERENCES

Abrams, J. R., & Giles, H. (2007). Ethnic identity gratifications selection and avoidance by African Americans: A group vitality and social identity gratifications perspective. *Media Psychology*, *9*(1), 115–134.

Allen, M., Emmers, T., Gebhardt, L., & Giery, M. A. (1995). Exposure to pornography and acceptance of rape myths. *Journal of Communication*, *45*(1), 5–26.

Ashcraft, B. (2010). How did Metroid's Samus Aran become a female character? *Kotaku.com*. http://kotaku.com/5634616/how-did-metroids-samus-aran-become-a-female-character

Aubrey, J. S., & Harrison, K. (2004). The gender-role content of children's favorite television programs and its links to their gender-related perceptions. *Media Psychology*, *6*(2), 111–146.

Bandura, A. (2001). Social cognitive theory: An agentic perspective. *Annual Review of Psychology*, *52*(1), 1–26.

Behm-Morawitz, E., & Mastro, D. E. (2008). Mean girls? The influence of gender portrayals in teen movies on emerging adults' gender-based attitudes and beliefs. *Journalism & Mass Communication Quarterly*, *85*(1), 131–146.

Billington, H. (2014). 10 most shockingly sexist video games. *The Richest.com*. http://www.therichest.com/rich-list/most-shocking/10-most-shockingly-sexist-video-games/?view=all

Bleakley, A., Hennessy, M., Fishbein, M., & Jordan, A. (2008). It works both ways: The relationship between exposure to sexual content in the media and adolescent sexual behavior. *Media Psychology*, *11*(4), 443–461.

Brown, J. D. (2000). Adolescents' sexual media diets. *Journal of Adolescent Health*, *27*(2), 35–40.

Brown, J. D. (2002). Mass media influences on sexuality. *Journal of Sex Research*, *39*(1), 42–45.

Brown, J. D., & L'Engle, K. L. (2009). X-rated sexual attitudes and behaviors associated with US early adolescents' exposure to sexually explicit media. *Communication Research*, *36*(1), 129–151.

Brown, J. D., L'Engle, K. L., Pardun, C. J., Guo, G., Kenneavy, K., & Jackson, C. (2006). Sexy media matter: Exposure to sexual content in music, movies, television, and magazines predicts black and white adolescents' sexual behavior. *Pediatrics*, *117*(4), 1018–1027.

Brown, J. D., Steele, J. R., & Walsh-Childers, K. (Eds.). (2001). *Sexual teens, sexual media: Investigating media's influence on adolescent sexuality*. New York: Routledge.

Brown Givens, S. M., & Monahan, J. L. (2005). Priming mammies, jezebels, and other controlling images: An examination of the influence of mediated stereotypes on perceptions of an African American woman. *Media Psychology*, *7*(1), 87–106.

Burgess, M. C., Dill, K. E., Stermer, S. P., Burgess, S. R., & Brown, B. P. (2011). Playing with prejudice: The prevalence and consequences of racial stereotypes in video games. *Media Psychology*, *14*(3), 289–311.

Campbell, C. (2013). Is porn right for games? *IGN.com*. http://www.ign.com/articles/2013/01/07/is-porn-right-for-games

Chalabaev, A., Sarrazin, P., Fontayne, P., Boiché, J., & Clément-Guillotin, C. (2013). The influence of sex stereotypes and gender roles on participation and performance in sport and exercise: Review and future directions. *Psychology of Sport and Exercise*, *14*(2), 136–144.

Coleman, R. (2011). Color blind: Race and the ethical reasoning of Blacks on journalism dilemmas. *Journalism & Mass Communication Quarterly*, *88*(2), 337–351.

Coleman, R. (2003). Race and ethical reasoning: The importance of race to journalistic decision making. *Journalism & Mass Communication Quarterly*, *80*(2), 295–310.

Dalisay, F., & Tan, A. (2009). Assimilation and contrast effects in the priming of Asian American and African American stereotypes through TV exposure. *Journalism & Mass Communication Quarterly*, *86*(1), 7–22.

Demby, G. (2014). 'Street Fighter II': Most racist nostalgic video game ever? *NPR.org*. http://www.npr.org/blogs/codeswitch/2014/03/16/290119728/street-fighter-ii-most-racist-nostalgic-video-game-ever

Dixon, T. L. (2006). Schemas as average conceptions: Skin tone, television news exposure, and culpability judgments. *Journalism & Mass Communication Quarterly*, 83(1), 131–149.

Elise, A. (2014). After 'Gamergate': The five most sexist video games of all time. *Ibtimes.com*. http://www.ibtimes.com/after-gamergate-five-most-sexist-video-games-all-time-1704905

Fiske, S. T. (1998). Stereotyping, prejudice, and discrimination. In Gilbert, Daniel T., Fiske, Susan T., Lindzey, Gardner. *The handbook of social psychology*. Volume Two (4th ed.). Boston: McGraw-Hill.

Fox, J., & Potocki, B. (2015). Lifetime video game consumption, interpersonal aggression, hostile sexism, and rape myth acceptance: A cultivation perspective. *Journal of Interpersonal Violence*, 0886260515570747.

Gerbner, G., Gross, L., Morgan, M., & Signorielli, N. (1986). Living with television: The dynamics of the cultivation process. *Perspectives on Media Effects*, 17–40.

Giantbomb.com (2014). Breast bounce. *Giantbomb.com*. http://www.giantbomb.com/breast-bounce/3015-96/

Haninger, K., & Thompson, K. M. (2004). Content and ratings of teen-rated video games. *Jama*, *291*(7), 856–865.

Harris, R. J., & Barlett, C. P. (2009) "Effects of Sex in the Media." In Bryant, J., & Oliver, M. B. (Eds.). (2009). *Media effects: Advances in theory and research*. New York: Routledge.

Hester, L. (2012). The 10 most racist video games. *Complex.com*. http://www.complex.com/pop-culture/2012/06/the-10-most-racist-video-games/#gallery

Huston, A. C., Wartella, E., & Donnerstein, E. (1998). Measuring the effects of sexual content in the media: A report to the Kaiser Family Foundation.

Ivory, J. D. (2006). Still a man's game: Gender representation in online reviews of video games. *Mass Communication & Society*, *9*(1), 103–114.

Juul, J. (2011). *Half-real: Video games between real rules and fictional worlds*. Cambridge, MA: MIT Press.

Klein, J. D., Brown, J. D., Dykers, C., Childers, K. W., Oliveri, J., & Porter, C. (1993). Adolescents' risky behavior and mass media use. *Pediatrics*, *92*(1), 24–31.

Knobloch-Westerwick, S., Appiah, O., & Alter, S. (2008). News selection patterns as a function of race: The discerning minority and the indiscriminating majority. *Media Psychology*, *11*(3), 400–417.

L'Engle, K. L., Brown, J. D., & Kenneavy, K. (2006). The mass media are an important context for adolescents' sexual behavior. *Journal of Adolescent Health*, *38*(3), 186–192.

Leone, M. (2014). Street Fighter II: An oral history. *Polygon.com*. http://www.polygon.com/a/street-fighter-2-oral-history

Link, B. G., & Phelan, J. C. (2001). Conceptualizing stigma. *Annual Review of Sociology*, 363–385.

MacCallum, M. (2008). *The Live Desk*. [Television broadcast]. New York: FOX News Channel.

Malamuth, N. M., & Briere, J. (1986). Sexual violence in the media: Indirect effects on aggression against women. *Journal of Social Issues*, *42*(3), 75–92.

Malamuth, N. M., & Check, J. V. (1981). The effects of mass media exposure on acceptance of violence against women: A field experiment. *Journal of Research in Personality*, *15*(4), 436–446.

Moore, M. (2009). Rapelay virtual rape game banned by Amazon. *Telegraph.co.uk*. http://www.telegraph.co.uk/technology/4611161/Rapelay-virtual-rape-game-banned-by-Amazon.html

Mullin, C. R., & Linz, D. (1995). Desensitization and resensitization to violence against women: effects of exposure to sexually violent films on judgments of domestic violence victims. *Journal of Personality and Social Psychology*, *69*(3), 449.

Oliver, M. B. (2003). African American men as "criminal and dangerous": Implications of media portrayals of crime on the "criminalization" of African American men. *Journal of African American Studies*, *7*(2), 3–18.

Pardun, C. J., L'Engle, K. L., & Brown, J. D. (2005). Linking exposure to outcomes: Early adolescents' consumption of sexual content in six media. *Mass Communication & Society*, *8*(2), 75–91.

Raith, G. (2012). 10 Most racist video games you will ever come across. *Gamingbolt.com*. http://gamingbolt.com/10-most-racist-video-games-you-will-ever-come-across

Ramasubramanian, S. (2011). The impact of stereotypical versus counter-stereotypical media exemplars on racial attitudes, causal attributions, and support for affirmative action. *Communication Research*, 38, 497–516.

Rivadeneyra, R., Ward, L. M., & Gordon, M. (2007). Distorted reflections: Media exposure and Latino adolescents' conceptions of self. *Media Psychology*, *9*(2), 261–290.

Rogers, R., & Liebler, C. (2015). Jubblies, mammaries, and boobs: Narratives of breast physics in video games. Presented at the annual conference of the International Communication Association, San Juan, Puerto Rico.

Rubin, A. M., West, D. V., & Mitchell, W. S. (2001). Differences in aggression, attitudes toward women, and distrust as reflected in popular music preferences. *Media Psychology*, *3*(1), 25–42.

Saleem, M., & Anderson, C. A. (2013). Arabs as terrorists: Effects of stereotypes within violent contexts on attitudes, perceptions, and affect. *Psychology of Violence*, *3*(1), 84.

Sargent, J.F. (2012). Top 10 weirdly racist video games. *Toptenz.net*. http://www.toptenz.net/top-10-weirdly-racist-video-games.php

Sowislo, J. F., & Orth, U. (2013). Does low self-esteem predict depression and anxiety? A meta-analysis of longitudinal studies. *Psychological Bulletin*, *139*(1), 213.

Steele, C. M., & Aronson, J. (1995). Stereotype threat and the intellectual test performance of African Americans. *Journal of Personality and Social Psychology*, *69*(5), 797.

Stermer, S. P., & Burkley, M. (2012). Xbox or SeXbox? An examination of sexualized content in video games. *Social and Personality Psychology Compass*, *6*(7), 525–535.

Stermer, S. P., & Burkley, M. (2015). SeX-Box: Exposure to sexist video games predicts benevolent sexism. *Psychology of Popular Media Culture*, *4*(1), 47.

Stevens, A. (2013). 10 blatantly sexist video games. *Whatculture.com*. http://whatculture.com/gaming/10-blatantly-sexist-video-games.php

Strasburger, V. C. (2012). Adolescents, sex, and the media. *Adolescent Medicine-State of the Art Reviews, 23*(1), 15.

The Week. (2009). Does 'gay elf' sex belong in videogames? *Theweek.com.* http://the-week.com/articles/498994/does-gay-elf-sex-belong-videogames

Thompson, K. M., & Haninger, K. (2001). Violence in E-rated video games. *JAMA, 286*(5), 591–598.

Thompson, K. M., Tepichin, K., & Haninger, K. (2006). Content and ratings of mature-rated video games. *Archives of Pediatrics & Adolescent Medicine, 160*(4), 402–410

Villani, S. (2001). Impact of media on children and adolescents: a 10-year review of the research. *Journal of the American Academy of Child & Adolescent Psychiatry, 40*(4), 392–401.

Walker, J. (2007). Lara Croft—NUDE! *Gamesradar.com.* http://www.gamesradar.com/lara-croft-nude/

Walsh, D. A., & Gentile, D. A. (2001). A validity test of movie, television, and video-game ratings. *Pediatrics, 107*(6), 1302–1308.

Williams, D., Martins, N., Consalvo, M., & Ivory, J. D. (2009). The virtual census: Representations of gender, race and age in video games. *New Media & Society, 11*(5), 815–834.

Yang, G. S., Huesmann, L. R., & Bushman, B. J. (2014). Effects of playing a violent video game as male versus female avatar on subsequent aggression in male and female players. *Aggressive Behavior, 40*(6), 537–541.

Yin-Poole, W. (2010). Team Ninja: If fans masturbate to DoA, that's a success. *Videogamer.com.* http://www.videogamer.com/psp/doa_paradise/news/team_ninja_if_fans_masturbate_to_doa_thats_a_success.html

Chapter Ten

Substance Use

In contemporary video games, it is not uncommon for a player's avatar to take painkillers, get drunk on virtual alcohol, or chug an energy drink (*Left for Dead 2*, *Dead Island*, and *Fallout 3* are recent popular examples). Oftentimes, in game play these virtual representations of substance use result in positive consequences for the players, such as "power-ups" or advantages over opponents. For example, painkillers and energy drinks increase speed and health while alcohol increases avatar strength. In other words, in-game substance use may enhance the players' ability to reach game goals and objectives.

Substance use is defined by the U.S. Department of Health and Human Services as "consumption of low or infrequent doses of alcohol and other drugs, sometimes called experimental, casual, or social use, such that damaging consequences may be rare or minor" (childwelfare.gov, 2009). According to studies, E (everyone) rated video games included a handful of instances of substance use (Thompson & Haninger, 2001) and in M (mature) rated games, 58 percent portrayed substance use (Thompson, Tepichin, & Haninger, 2006).

While the work of Thompson and colleagues studied the occurrence of substance use, the studies are dated and it is possible that these content analyses omitted instances of substance use by using an overly narrow conceptualization. Substance use in these instances was limited to alcohol, tobacco, and illicit drugs. Because of the fictionalized and fanciful nature of many video games, substance use can easily be expanded beyond actual substances (e.g., cigarettes, alcohol, street drugs, etc.) to fantasy substances. These substances, such as a magic potion, for example, symbolize the use of substances to enhance or alter experiences of the users. In other words, the rules of video games are not bound by the same rules of the physical world and interpretations of video game content should be calibrated to do so.

In video games, substance use can have positive effects (enhanced speed), negative effects (loss of health), or neutral effects (no discernible advantages or disadvantages). Social cognitive theory argues that media characters serve as models for audience members (Bandura, 1986, 2002, 2004; Denler, Wolters, & Benzon, 2013). If audiences observe a mediated character behaving a certain way and experiencing positive consequences (or no negative consequences), this positive reinforcement improves attitudes toward that behavior and can increase the likelihood of imitation of the behavior. As a result, this book suggests that substance use be analyzed based on the rules of the game (does it play by fantasy rules or realistic rules?) and its feedback (what is the outcome of the substance use, positive or negative?).

In terms of the rules, mediated content does not have to be highly realistic to be influential to users (Sherry, 2001). For instance, Krcmar and Curtis (2003) found that consuming media with fantasy violence led children to judge subsequent uses of violence as morally acceptable. Consequently, noting the occurrences of fantasy substances in popular video games is important because many video games take place in fantasy realms. Thus, substance use in video games may not be accurately captured by only measuring the occurrence of real world substances. There may be no alcohol known as vodka in a futuristic video game. However, an avatar might order a fictional alcoholic or otherwise intoxicating drink in a space-age tavern. Or, a game may feature an orc (i.e., an ugly, war-prone, fantasy creature) in a fantasy game who drinks mind-altering potions in a medieval pub. Alternatively, a game might take place in a realistic war with a human soldier but the soldier may use a fictional injection to give him- or herself super speed or strength. Importantly, content analyses account for fantasy violence when coding for the amount of violence in video games; however, in video game content analyses there has not yet been an account of uses of fantasy substances (Haninger, Ryan, & Thompson, 2004; Hartmann, Krakowiak, & Tsay-Vogel, 2014; Thompson & Haninger, 2001; Thompson et al., 2006) despite a lack of theoretical grounding for this omission. By not doing so, some content of interest is going unanalyzed, particularly depictions of all fictional substances in current games with separate characterizations of positive and negative outcomes.

Interactivity/feedback is another important mechanism to be considered when studying video games. Interactivity and feedback can influence people's attitudes toward content, feelings of presence, engagement with content, and retention of content, often increasing each (Ariely, 2000; Biocca, Harms, & Burgoon, 2003; Reeves & Read, 2009; Sundar & Kim, 2005; Teo, Oh, Liu, & Wei, 2003). For example, Teo et al. (2003) found that higher levels of interactivity resulted in increased perceptions of satisfaction, effectiveness, efficiency, value, and overall attitude toward a website. Thus, inter-active substance use might invoke positive attitudes toward substance use content, higher levels of engagement with substance use content, and better retention of substance use content. In addition, video games are of particular import because players are more likely to identify with, or assume the role of the character using the substance through self-presentation (Klimmt, Hefner, & Vorderer, 2009; Lewis, Weber, & Bowman, 2008; Peña, Hancock, & Merola, 2009; Yee & Bailenson, 2007; Yee, Bailenson, & Ducheneaut, 2009). Therefore, it is important to note whether or not a video game player's character—someone the player may already identify with—is the one per-forming the substance use or if the player is instead passively observing the substance use of another character.

Based on aforementioned theoretical foundations and empirical evidence, an updated content analysis of substance use in video games is necessary to more accurately describe in-game substance use. Accordingly, a content analysis was used to answer the following questions with special attention to rules, feedback, and self-presentation: How much more prevalent is sub-stance use in video games when accounting for fictional substances than when only counting non-fictional substances? How are consequences of sub-stance use portrayed in video games (positively, negatively, or neutrally)? How often does the player representatively use a substance?

To answer these questions, a content analysis was performed that exam-ined the worldwide top 44 selling video games from recent years for portray-als of substance use (Rogers, Myrick, Kalyanaraman, & White, 2012). These games were aggregated for four gaming consoles: Nintendo's Wii (Wii), Sony's Play Station 3 (PS3), Microsoft's Xbox 360 (Xbox 360), and the Nintendo DS. The worldwide sales numbers on vgchartz.com, a source cited by the *New York Times* (Muskus, 2008), *Forbes* (Noer, 2008), and the BBC (Reed, 2008), identified the highest selling games for each year in the sam-ple. Thus, these games are the most popular and most played games for this generation.

In cases where the same title appeared multiple times as a best seller, only one version of the title was coded. For example, *Call of Duty Modern War-fare 2* was a top selling game for Xbox 360, PS3, and Wii for multiple years in the sample. Only one version per title was considered in this content analysis.

Coders recorded each occurrence of substance use in each session of play. This content analysis adopted the U.S. Department of Health and Human Services' definition of substance use (childwelfare.gov, 2009) but extended it to video games such that a video game character used the substance. Objects that were used in a fashion analogous to known substances were coded (smoked, injected, consumed, etc.). If the object was readily identifiable as an innocuous object or normal food, like drinking water or a turkey leg, then it was not coded as substance use. Coders also measured whether or not the substance use could be considered medical in nature. For example, a medical gel in *Mass Effect* helps restore health in a life or death scenario and a shot of morphine in *Call of Duty* might be used to aid a severely wounded character. Their medical nature makes them more akin to traditional health care and different than other substance uses harmful to health or even illegal in the real world. These portrayals of substance can subtly promote the use of substances, be they medicinal or illicit, as a way to overcome barriers. Indeed, there has been a shift to medicalization of society, where individuals turn to substances to solve problems instead of turning to behavioral solutions (Chodoff, 2002). As a result, it is important to study all substance use because it establishes a pattern of substance need to succeed in a game (or life) instead of relying on skill, perseverance, etc.

If substance use was present, then the coder recorded a series of other variables relating to the substance use. The coder noted if the use was part of a game play sequence or included in a narrative scene. In game play sequences, the player had a degree of control over some portions of the game. In narrative scenes, the player did not have control over the game and these sections were not interactive. Thus, coding for this indicated if aspects of the substance use occurrence were under the player's control or not.

Other variables coded for included: the nature of the substance used as realistic or fantasy, the nature of the game as real or fantasy, and the nature of the player's avatar as human or other. Realistic substance uses included alcohol, cigarettes, or otherwise identifiable real-world substances, while fantasy substance use was considered a fictional substance that exists in a game universe but does not exist in the physical world. An example would be an alien tonic or a magical elixir.

Coders also indicated if the player's avatar was the one using the substance or if it was another game character or avatar. This distinction was used to measure whether or not a representation of the self was using the substance. The coders also indicated if the outcome of the substance use was portrayed as positive, negative, or neutral. A positive portrayal was defined as one that helped gamers complete game objectives. For example, taking a pill that makes an avatar invisible so it can sneak into the enemy's secret lair would be coded as a positive portrayal. Negative portrayals were defined as those hindering players' completion of game objectives. For example, drinking alcohol in certain games makes the controls less responsive and the game more difficult to complete successfully. Neutral portrayals were defined as having no noticeable effects on game play or the positive and negative effects on game play were balanced. For example, a non-player character smoking a cigar in the background who is purely aesthetic and has no bearing on game play would be a neutral portrayal. Another example of a neutral portrayal would be a player's avatar drinking alcohol that makes the avatar stronger while simultaneously making the avatar harder to control. Note this does not address narrative consequences of substance use, normative values of substance use, nor any health consequences, only game play consequences.

Of the 44 games coded, 30 games (68.2%) were rated E for everyone, 1 game (2.3%) was rated T for Teen, and 13 games (29.5%) were rated M for mature. No games were rated AO (adults only). Twenty-two of the games (50.0%) featured some form of substance use while the remaining 22 (50.0%) featured no occurrences of substance use. Within the 22 games with portrayals of substance use, there were 190 occurrences. Instances of substance use ranged from 1 second to 122 seconds for a total of 1,234 seconds or 20.56 minutes.

The prevalence of substance use in video games when accounting for fictional substances, not just realistic substances, went up considerably. In this sample, there were 57 realistic portrayals of substance use, including but not limited to the use of painkillers, smoking tobacco, and drinking alcohol. Realistic portrayals accounted for 30.0% of the total occurrences of substance use. Meanwhile, there were 133 fictional portrayals of substance use, such as consuming potions, power pellets, or using spray antidotes. These portrayals accounted for 70.0% of the total occurrences. In this sample, fictional portrayals of substance use were more than twice as common as realistic portrayals. This highlights the importance of accounting for fantastical rules in video game content analyses of substance use. The body and mind often react to fiction in the same manner they react to fact, simulating what it would be like for one to encounter a stimuli in the real world (Paul, 2012; Zillmann & Knobloch, 2001). Thus, viewing fictional or fantasy instances of substance use could have similar effects as viewing realistic ones. The effects of fantasy substance use on video game players is worth noting as fantasy content has been shown to influence audience members (Krcmar & Curtis, 2003; Parker & Lepper, 1992). Given that fantasy substance use in this study of the currently most popular video games was nearly twice as prevalent as real substance use, future research should test the effects of such use on various ages of game players. The rules of many video games place the player into a realistic or fantasy setting. Since rules are such an important factor in video games, this is a critical inclusion for research on video games, especially since the distinction provides disparate results.

Substance uses were portrayed with largely positive consequences in these video games. One hundred fifty-seven (82.6%) of the occurrences were positive. In other words, 157 of the occurrences of substance use helped players accomplish in-game goals. Meanwhile, there were 31 (16.3%) occurrences when substance use was neutral to the achievement of in-game goals. Lastly, there were only 2 (1.0%) occurrences of substance use where use of the substance hindered the achievement of in-game goals. The neutral occurrences were largely aesthetic as most took place during narrative sequences with no impact on game play (29, 93.5%) and only two had balanced positive and negative effects (6.4%). There was also a significant difference in valence of the portrayals of substance use between fantasy and realistic uses. For realistic portrayals of substance use, most portrayals were neutral (93.1%) while for fantasy portrayals, substance use was almost always positive in valence (96.3%).

The portrayal of substance use in this video game sample was overwhelmingly positive but much of that was explained by the medical nature of substance use in video games. Sixty-seven (35.3%) of the occurrences were medical in nature, while 123 (64.7%) were considered non-medical. When removing medical occurrences of substance use, 93 (48.9%) of the occurrences were positive and non-medical. Through the lens of feedback and social cognitive theory, this finding would predict that players observing positive consequences of substance use may be more likely to adopt positive attitudes of the behavior (Bandura, 2002). Obviously, this statement cannot be affirmed by an analysis of content alone, but future experiment work could provide support for this prediction. In this case, substance use behaviors were typically rewarded and not punished. Thus, the substance use behaviors were encouraged by the feedback loop.

Substance use portrayals tended to also be under the player's control in these video games. In this sample, 161 (84.7%) of the occurrences of substance use occurred during game play sequences, while 29 (15.3%) occurrences happened during narrative, passive sequences. In other words, a majority of the occurrences took place when players had some degree of control over the content. That control could mean that the substance use was performed by the player or some other uncontrolled character. One hundred forty-eight (77.9%) occurrences of substance use were performed by the player's avatar and 42 (22.1%) occurrences of substance use were performed by another non-player avatar. There were 140 (73.7%) occurrences that were both performed by the player's avatar and happened during a game play sequence. These occurrences were controlled by the player and were performed by the avatar. That means that the player representatively took the substance 73.7 percent of the time. Given the ability of content control to influence attitudes (Ariely, 2000; Sundar & Kim, 2005; Teo et al., 2003), this finding points to the possibility that these substance uses may amplify the effects predicted by social cognitive theory. These occurrences of substance use may be more influential than passive occurrences within the games, or within other mediated contexts. This supposition of increased influence of interactively modeled substance use behaviors has implications for how health communication researchers think about the effects of media messages on individuals' substance use behaviors. It is possible that even if audiences see anti-drug or other anti-substance use messages in traditional mass media formats, video game players, especially heavy players of the games with the most substance use, may be less influenced by the healthy but passive message than by their immersive video game experience. Health-related video games targeting heavy game users could be an effective way to counteract these pro-substance use experiences in current top-selling games. Encouraging the makers of top-selling games to consider the possible effects of their content may be a more practical route to take for those working to treat or prevent substance use. While content producers have the right to create games as they see fit, the information in this study is likely of interest to those who are concerned with possible negative consequences of game design. If content producers are interested in altering practices based on these findings, they should consider including more clarity while describing substances in the games as well as thinking carefully about the in-game consequences of the substance use.

Lastly, all of the games in the sample featured human avatars, though some games had options to be non-human. For example, *Super Smash Brothers Brawl* allows players to select from a variety of avatars, some human and some not. In spite of this, the games in this sample mostly fit into a fantasy setting (N = 161, 84.74%) and less than one-fifth (N = 29) of the games portrayed realistic settings (15.26%). This means that the character in the game could be more closely related to the player through self-presentation than if it had been a non-human. If the player identifies with his or her avatar, as previous research has found likely, then he or she would be more likely to emulate substance use behaviors (Klimmt et al., 2009; Klimmt, Hefner, Vorderer, Roth, & Blake, 2010). Identifying with an avatar that uses a substance could lead to a shift in players' self concepts as drug users (Comello & Slater, 2011).

Ultimately, this chapter suggests that instances of substance use in video games are much more common—after accounting for fictional substances—than perhaps previously thought. This finding should inform conceptualizations of future measures of substance use in video games in order to acknowledge the fantasy setting of many games. Overall, the portrayals of substance use were overwhelmingly positive and thus, based on social cognitive theory and the understanding of feedback, may encourage positive attitudes toward substance use behaviors (Bandura, 1986, 2002, 2004). Similarly, portrayals of substance use were often under the player's control and thus might be even more influential than passive portrayals. Finally, the many instances of substance use portrayals by the player's own avatars have important implications for media effects through the lens of self-presentation. The findings detailed in this chapter could be used to raise awareness among researchers, consumers, parents, and content producers who may be concerned about the effects of video games on users.

REFERENCES

Ariely, D. (2000). Controlling the information flow: Effects on consumers' decision making and preferences. *Journal of Consumer Research, 27*(2), 233–248.

Bandura, A. (1986). *Social foundations of thought and action: A social cognitive theory.* Englewood Cliffs, NJ: Prentice-Hall.

Bandura, A. (2002). Social cognitive theory of mass communication. *Media Effects.* Mahwah, NJ: Lawrence Erlbaum Associates, Publishers.

Bandura, A. (2004). Health promotion by social cognitive means. *Health Education & Behavior, 31*(2), 143–164.

Biocca, F., Harms, C., & Burgoon, J. K. (2003). Toward a more robust theory and measure of social presence: Review and suggested criteria. *PRESENCE: Teleoperators & Virtual Environments, 12*, 456–480.

Childwelfare.gov (2009). Protecting children in families affected by substance use disorders. *Childwelfare.gov.* https://www.childwelfare.gov/pubs/usermanuals/substanceuse/appendixa.cfm

Chodoff, P. (2002). The medicalization of the human condition. *Psychiatric Services, 53*(5), 627–628.

Comello, M. L. G., & Slater, M. D. (2011). The effects of drug-prevention messages on the accessibility of identity-related constructs. *Journal of Health Communication, 16*(5), 458–469.

Denler, H., Wolters, C., & Benzon, M. (2013). Social cognitive theory. *Education.com.*

Haninger, K. M., Ryan, S. & Thompson, K. M. (2004). Violence in teen-rated video games. *Medscape General Medicine, 6*(1): 1.

Hartmann, T., Krakowiak, K. M., & Tsay-Vogel, M. (2014). How violent video games communicate violence: A literature review and content analysis of moral disengagement factors. *Communication Monographs, 81*(3), 310–332.

Klimmt, C., Hefner, D., & Vorderer, P. (2009). The video game experience as "true" identification: A theory of enjoyable alterations of players' self-perception. *Communication Theory* (10503293), 19(4), 351–373.

Klimmt, C., Hefner, D., Vorderer, P., Roth, C., & Blake, C. (2010). Identification with video game characters as automatic shift of self-perceptions. *Media Psychology, 13*(4), 323–338.

Krcmar, M. & Curtis, S. (2003). Mental models: The impact of fantasy violence on children's moral reasoning. *Journal of Communication, 53*(3), 460–478.

Lewis, M. L., Weber, R., & Bowman, N. (2008). "They may be pixels, but they're MY pixels": Developing a metric of character attachment in role-playing video games. *Cyberpsychology & Behavior, 11*(4), 515–518.

Muskus, J. (2008). New Wii games find a big (but stingy) audience. *NYTimes.com.* http://www.nytimes.com/2008/04/21/technology/21wii.html?_r=1&ref=business

Noer, M. (2008). The future of video games. *Forbes.com.* http://www.forbes.com/2008/02/08/future-video-games-tech-future07-cx_mn_de_0211game.html

Parker, L. E., & Lepper, M. R. (1992). Effects of fantasy contexts on children's learningand motivation: Making learning more fun. *Journal of Personality and Social Psychology, 62*(4), 625–633.

Paul, A. M. (2012). Your brain on fiction. *NYTimes.com.* http://www.nytimes.com/2012/03/18/opinion/sunday/the-neuroscience-of-yourbrain-on-fiction.html?_r=1&src=me&ref=general

Peña, J., Hancock, J. T., & Merola, N. A. (2009). The priming effects of avatars in virtual settings. *Communication Research, 36*(6), 838–856.

Reed, J. (2008). Xbox 360 to get UK price cut. *BBC.co.uk.* http://news.bbc.co.uk/newsbeat/hi/newsbeat/newsid_7618000/7618515.stm

Reeves, B., & Read, J. L. (2009). *Total engagement: Using games and virtual worlds to change the way people work and businesses compete* (195–196). Boston, MA: Harvard Business Press.

Rogers, R., Myrick, J., Kalyanaraman, S., & White, E. (2012). *Pills and power-ups: Substance use in video games.* Presented at the annual conference of the Association for Education in Journalism and Mass Communication, Chicago, IL.

Sherry, J. L. (2001). The effects of violent video games on aggression. *Human Communication Research, 27*(3), 409–431.

Sundar, S. S., & Kim, J. (2005). Interactivity and persuasion: Influencing attitudes with information and involvement. *Journal of Interactive Advertising, 5*(2), 6–29.

Teo, H. H., Oh, L. B., Liu, C., & Wei, K. K. (2003). An empirical study of the effects of interactivity on Web user attitude. *International Journal of Human Computer Studies, 58*, 281–305.

Thompson, K. M., & Haninger, K. (2001). Violence in E-rated video games. *JAMA, 286*, 591–598.

Thompson, K. M., Tepichin, K., & Haninger, K. (2006). Content and ratings of mature rated video games. *Archives of Pediatrics & Adolescent Medicine 160*(4), 402–410.

Vgchartz.com (2014). Global yearly chart. *VGChartz.com.* Retrieved from: http://www.vgchartz.com/yearly/2006/Global/

Yee, N., & Bailenson, J. (2007). The proteus effect: The effect of transformed selfrepresentation on behaviour. *Human Communication Research, 33*(3), 271–290.

Yee, N., Bailenson, J. N., & Ducheneaut, N. (2009). The Proteus effect: Implications of transformed digital self-representation on online and offline behavior. *Communication Research, 36*(2), 285–312.

Zillmann, D., & Knobloch, S. (2001). Emotional reactions to narratives about the fortunes of personae in the news theater. *Poetics, 29*(3), 189–206.

Chapter Eleven

Obesity/Depression

Obesity and depression are linked in many cases (Brooks, 2010; Lawson, 2003). Their interrelation suggests that one can cause the other and vice versa, such that obesity can cause one to become depressed and being depressed can cause one to become obese. Not surprisingly, mental health issues and physical health issues are often related. In this case, this book discusses them in conjunction because depression and obesity are also often linked to video game play.

In both the popular press and scholarly research, video games have been linked to obesity and depression. Within the last few years, the popular press has run the following headlines:

- Video game "addiction" tied to depression, anxiety in kids (Gordon, 2011)
- Do videogames make depression worse? (Owen, 2012)
- Do video games contribute to childhood obesity? (Loop, 2013)
- TV, video games linked to obesity (Kelly, 2012)
- Are TV and video games making kids fat? (Sanghavi, 2012)
- Overload of screen time "causes depression in children." (Burrell, 2013)
- Less sleep, more time online raise risk for teen depression (Singh, 2014)

The argument is fairly intuitive: Video games can be isolating such that an individual may play a video game by him- or herself instead of socializing with friends or family. This isolation and lack of social interaction can lead to depression. Likewise, video games encourage players to be sedentary for extended periods of time. An individual might sit on the couch to play a video game instead of going to the gym for aerobic exercise or playing outside. This would result in weight gain and eventually obesity. The two concerns then work in compound with one another to make obesity and depression worse. One article argues that this is a particularly compelling issue because video games create a group of children who are at high risk for mental illness, but are not highly visible because they do not display typical signs of antisocial behavior such as aggression or substance abuse (Singh, 2014).

Depression has been defined as a negative emotion resulting in extreme sadness and an inability to perform certain tasks (Russoniello, O'Brien, & Parks, 2009). According to the World Health Organization, more than 350 million people suffer from depression. It has been noted that longitudinal effects of video game play may be related to depression such that those who play a large degree of video games tend to be more depressed while those, over time, who played fewer video games tend to be less depressed (Bavelier, Green, Han, Renshaw, Merzenich, & Gentile, 2011). Another study confirmed that those who played video games had higher levels of depression than their non-gaming counterparts (Mentzoni et al., 2011) such that as playing time increased, so did levels of depression (Wenzel, Bakken, Johansson, Götestam, & Øren, 2009). Similarly, players of *Everquest 2*, a MMORPG, tended to suffer from mental illness in the form of high levels of depression (Williams, Yee, & Caplan, 2008). According to Gentile and colleagues (2011) roughly 9 percent of the population plays video game pathologically and prolonged pathological video game play is associated with depression. Further complicating this issue, different video games might elicit different emotional responses. For example, in one experiment certain video games elicited high feelings of depression while others did not (Ravaja et al., 2004). The authors speculate that this was due to the low quality of the game. In other words, a game that is not fun to play can lead to negative emotional states that resemble depression. Following this logic conversely, if a game is fun, it should lead to fewer emotions that resemble depression. Thus, the extent of depression elicited by a video game might be directly related to the quality of its rules and feedback. Notably, few of these studies specifically argue that video games are *causing* depression. Rather, it is more likely that video games may contribute to depressive states.

Based on the preceding evidence, one might conclude that video games are closely tied to depression. However, a closer examination of the literature reveals a lack of consensus on this topic. Cross-sectional and longitudinal data suggest that video game play is not a strong predictor of depression (Ferguson, Garza, Jerabeck, Ramos, & Galindo, 2013). Meanwhile, another study suggested that depression was associated with television viewing and many other antisocial behaviors such as aggression, crime, rule-breaking, and bullying, but not video games (Ferguson, San Miguel, & Hartley, 2009). Yet, another study confirmed that video game play, as well as excess time spent playing a video game, was not associated with depression (Valadez & Ferguson, 2012). Some evidence even suggests that video games might actually decrease negative emotions such as depression (Ferguson & Rueda, 2010). When players are depressed, as induced by a frustration task, playing a video game might serve to repair that state and decrease the level of depression (Han, Hwang, & Renshaw, 2010). In that fashion, it is speculated that video games could be therapeutic for those who suffer from depression (Kutner & Olson, 2008) and a study measuring brain waves using EEG technology showed that video games can alter brain waves in order to decrease depression (Russoniello et al., 2009). The underlying mechanism here is likely quality feedback. If someone is depressed, or more specifically frustrated to the degree that it resembles depression, an effective feedback loop can make a player feel competent, capable of reaching goals, and effective. These outcomes might serve to correct negative mood states related to depression.

Similarly, obesity has been associated with video game use (Stettler, Signer, & Suter, 2004; Vandewater, Shim, & Caplovitz, 2004) such that more time playing video games is related to less physical activity and a decrease in energy expenditure (Bhadoria, Kapil, & Kaur, 2015; Carvalhal, Padez, Moreira, & Rosado, 2007). Obesity is an unhealthy proportion of fat in the body. According to the Centers for Disease Control, obesity in the United States has grown exponentially in the past 30 years (Kelly, 2012). Notably, this 30-year period coincides with the growth of the video game industry and its entry into the mainstream, with some of the earliest popular video games releasing in the 1970s. This, in conjunction with the fact that sitting on the couch while playing a video game is associated with snacking, exacerbates obesity concerns as related to video games (Kelly, 2012). And the sorts of households that tend to not regulate the amount of time a child plays video games is also likely the type of household that does not regulate a child's diet (Sanghavi, 2012) further compounding the issue.

Individuals who play video games tend to be heavier than those that do not (Stettler et al., 2004; Vandewater et al., 2004). Indeed, while slightly less than the American average, *Everquest 2* players are overweight (Williams et al., 2008). However, again, the results of these studies are not always consistent. One area of inquiry suggests that video games can actually serve to combat obesity (Thompson et al., 2008). With the trend of motion controls in video games, active video games or exergames have become more prevalent and these games can make players more active, not less (Maddison et al., 2011; Mhurchu et al., 2008). A meta-analysis of studies examining physical activity in video games showed that if a video game encourages a large degree of physical activity, then it may be associated with decreased obesity (Guy, Ratzki-Leewing, & Gwadry-Sridhar, 2011).

This literature, examined in combination, shows that video game play, depression, and obesity are intertwined in ways that have not yet been fully parsed. Accordingly, pathological video game play is likely comorbid with depression and obesity (Gordon, 2011; Owen, 2012), especially when look-ing at longitudinal game play. In summary, the studies suggest that these three issues likely feed off of one another.

Pathological video game play might be understood as video game addic-tion such that video game players can become addicted to games to the degree that game play interferes with a healthy and productive lifestyle. Addiction is defined as a pleasurable activity that is continued despite nega-tive consequences and a lack of control over continued behavior (Goodman, 1990). Then, video game addiction is a persistent pattern of video game play that interrupts daily life (King, Delfabbro, & Griffiths, 2013). In 2013, the American Psychological Association provided guidelines for assessing Inter-net gaming addiction (Petry et al., 2014). These guidelines include but are not limited to:

• Do you feel restless, irritable, moody, angry, anxious, or sad when at-tempting to cut down or stop gaming, or when you are unable to play?
• Do you feel the need to play for increasing amounts of time, play more exciting games, or use more powerful equipment to get the same amount of excitement you used to get?
• Do you feel that you should play less, but are unable to cut back on the amount of time you spend playing games?
• Do you lose interest in or reduce participation in other recreational activ-ities (hobbies, meetings with friends) due to gaming?
• Do you continue to play games even though you are aware of negative consequences, such as not getting enough sleep, being late to school/work, spending too much money, having arguments with others, or neglecting important duties?
• Do you game to escape from or forget about personal problems, or to relieve uncomfortable feelings such as guilt, anxiety, helplessness, or de-pression?
• Do you risk or lose significant relationships, or job, educational, or career opportunities because of gaming?

These questions detail issues related to things such as tolerance, preoccu-pation, and withdrawal. Notably, many of these items may be related to obesity and depression. For example, the first item references negative emo-tional states closely related to depression. And other items refer to not partic-ipating in recreational activities or neglecting important duties because of video games. In this instance, these activities and duties could be exercise, something that pathological video game players could miss which can con-tribute to obesity. Despite these criteria, video game addiction was not and is not officially recognized by the *Diagnostic and Statistical Manual of Mental Disorders*, the guidelines for diagnosing psychiatric disorders (Petry et al.,

2014). To be clear, Internet gaming disorder was included but not gaming disorder "because of the distinguishing features and increased risks of clinically significant problems associated with gaming in particular" (Petry et al., 2014, p. 2).

One resistance to this classification as addiction is that behavior disorders should not be conflated with substance use disorders (Petry et al., 2014). Wood (2008) argues that the term "addiction" is inaccurately applied to video games because video games do not actually have any addictive properties. Regardless of these arguments, video games are often referred to as addictive in common parlance. One video game journalist even referred to the video game *Star Wars: The Old Republic* as his "morphine" that provided comfort and escape during a difficult period of his life (Owen, 2012). Another popular press article stated plainly, "violent video games can be as addicting as drugs" (Miller, 2013). Perhaps these claims are appropriate as fMRI data suggests that pathological video game play activates the brain similarly to substance use (Han et al., 2010).

While there are a handful of exceptions (Skoric, Teo, & Neo, 2009; Wood, 2008), there appears to be a strong agreement in the research community regarding the nature of video game addiction. Video game addiction is shown to be associated with aggression, relationship issues, and poor academic performance (Chiu, Lee, & Huang, 2004; Gentile et al., 2011; Grüsser, Thalemann, & Griffiths, 2006; Hauge & Gentile, 2003; Ng & Wiemer-Hastings, 2005). And people who are addicted to video games become desensitized to dopamine responses related to their game play (Weinstein, 2010).

The suggestion is that video games are likely related to depression and obesity, but the relationship may be much more complex than straightforward causality. One way to understand this relationship might be in terms of a feedback loop. It has been speculated that depression, obesity, and video game play interact and create a "negative" feedback loop (Owen, 2012). That is, obesity may lead to more game play which may lead to more weight gain and ultimately more depression. Or video game play may lead to weight gain which leads to depression which leads to more video game play. The feedback of the game itself might contribute to these issues as well. Video game feedback is designed to feel satisfying. Effective video game feedback, and effective feedback in general, motivates people to continue pursuit of a goal. Thus, players are encouraged to stay in front of video games, cutting themselves off socially and, assuming the game is not an active game, reducing physical activity.

Also, in terms of self-presentation, a player might generate misconceptions of him- or herself based on the avatars they are using. Indeed, many of the characters in video games are active. In *Madden*, the characters are highly athletic. In *Call of Duty* the characters are highly trained soldiers. Consequently, the player may perceive him or herself as more active than he or she actually is because they are psychologically merging with active characters. This could contribute to weight gain. Likewise, a character in a game might be highly social, as in *The Sims* or *World of Warcraft*. A player might perceive these mediated interactions as adequate while the player is actually quite isolated socially in the physical world.

In summary, there is a degree of evidence that video games are related to depression and obesity. Despite the lack of an official recognition of video game addiction, the research community will continue to develop an understanding of this complex issue. In that vein, feedback and self-presentation are germane areas of exploration when examining the relationship between video games, depression, and obesity.

REFERENCES

Bavelier, D., Green, C. S., Han, D. H., Renshaw, P. F., Merzenich, M. M., & Gentile, D. A. (2011). Brains on video games. *Nature Reviews Neuroscience, 12*(12), 763–768.

Bhadoria, A. S., Kapil, U., & Kaur, S. (2015). Association of duration of time spent on television, computer and video games with obesity amongst children in National Capital territory of Delhi. *International Journal of Preventive Medicine, 1*(2).

Brooks, M. (2010). Obesity and depression are a two-way street. *Reuters.com*. http://www.reuters.com/article/2010/03/04/us-obesity-depression-idUSTRE6234RF20100304

Burrell, I. (2013). Overload of screen time 'causes depression in children.' *Independent.co.uk*. http://www.independent.co.uk/life-style/health-and-families/health-news/overload-of-screen-time-causes-depression-in-children-8786826.html

Carvalhal, M. M., Padez, M. C., Moreira, P. A., & Rosado, V. M. (2007). Overweight and obesity related to activities in Portuguese children, 7–9 years. *The European Journal of Public Health, 17*(1), 42–46.

Chiu, S. I., Lee, J. Z., & Huang, D. H. (2004). Video game addiction in children and teenagers in Taiwan. *CyberPsychology & Behavior, 7*(5), 571–581.

Ferguson, C. J., Garza, A., Jerabeck, J., Ramos, R., & Galindo, M. (2013). Not worth the fuss after all? Cross-sectional and prospective data on violent video game influences on aggression, visuospatial cognition and mathematics ability in a sample of youth. *Journal of Youth and Adolescence, 42*(1), 109–122.

Ferguson, C. J., & Rueda, S. M. (2010). The Hitman study: Violent video game exposure effects on aggressive behavior, hostile feelings, and depression. *European Psychologist, 15*(2), 99.

Ferguson, C. J., San Miguel, C., & Hartley, R. D. (2009). A multivariate analysis of youth violence and aggression: the influence of family, peers, depression, and media violence. *The Journal of Pediatrics, 155*(6), 904–908.

Gentile, D. A., Choo, H., Liau, A., Sim, T., Li, D., Fung, D., & Khoo, A. (2011). Pathological video game use among youths: a two-year longitudinal study. *Pediatrics, 127*(2), e319–e329.

Goodman, A. (1990). Addiction: definition and implications. *British Journal of Addiction, 85*(11), 1403–1408.

Gordon, S. (2011). Video game 'addiction' tied to depression, anxiety in kids. *Usnews.com*. http://health.usnews.com/health-news/family-health/brain-and-behavior/articles/2011/01/17/video-game-addiction-tied-to-depression-anxiety-in-kids

Grüsser, S. M., Thalemann, R., & Griffiths, M. D. (2006). Excessive computer game playing: evidence for addiction and aggression? *CyberPsychology & Behavior, 10*(2), 290–292.

Guy, S., Ratzki-Leewing, A., & Gwadry-Sridhar, F. (2011). Moving beyond the stigma: systematic review of video games and their potential to combat obesity. *International Journal of Hypertension*, 2011.

Han, D. H., Hwang, J. W., & Renshaw, P. F. (2010). Bupropion sustained release treatment decreases craving for video games and cue-induced brain activity in patients with Internet video game addiction. *Experimental and Clinical Psychopharmacology*, *18*(4), 297.

Hauge, M. R., & Gentile, D. A. (2003, April). Video game addiction among adolescents: Associations with academic performance and aggression. In Society for Research in Child Development Conference.

Kelly, J. (2012). TV, video games linked to obesity. *Post-Gazette*. http://www.post-gazette.com/news/health/2012/11/12/TV-video-games-linked-to-obesity/stories/201211120171

King, D., Delfabbro, P., & Griffiths, M. (2013). Video game addiction.

Kutner, L., & Olson, C. (2008). *Grand theft childhood: The surprising truth about violent video games and what parents can do*. New York: Simon and Schuster.

Lawson, W. (2003). The Obesity-Depression Link. *PsychologyToday.com*. https://www.psychologytoday.com/articles/200305/the-obesity-depression-link

Loop, E. (2013). Do video games contribute to childhood obesity? *Livestrong.com*. http://www.livestrong.com/article/376383-obesity-in-children-video-games/

Maddison, R., Foley, L., Mhurchu, C. N., Jiang, Y., Jull, A., Prapavessis, H., & Rodgers, A. (2011). Effects of active video games on body composition: a randomized controlled trial. *The American Journal of Clinical Nutrition*, *94*(1), 156–163.

Mentzoni, R. A., Brunborg, G. S., Molde, H., Myrseth, H., Skouverøe, K. J. M., Hetland, J., & Pallesen, S. (2011). Problematic video game use: estimated prevalence and associations with mental and physical health. *Cyberpsychology, Behavior, and Social Networking*, *14*(10), 591–596.

Mhurchu, C. N., Maddison, R., Jiang, Y., Jull, A., Prapavessis, H., & Rodgers, A. (2008). Couch potatoes to jumping beans: A pilot study of the effect of active video games on physical activity in children. *International Journal of Behavioral Nutrition and Physical Activity*, *5*(1), 8.

Miller, T. (2013). Video game addiction and other Internet compulsive disorders mask depression, anxiety, learning disabilities. *Nydailynews.com*. http://www.nydailynews.com/lifestyle/health/kids-addicted-video-games-violent-experts-article-1.1298338

Ng, B. D., & Wiemer-Hastings, P. (2005). Addiction to the internet and online gaming. *CyberPsychology & Behavior*, *8*(2), 110–113.

Owen, P. (2012). Do videogames make depression worse? *Kotaku.com*. http://kotaku.com/5992636/do-video-games-make-depression-worse

Petry, N. M., Rehbein, F., Gentile, D. A., Lemmens, J. S., Rumpf, H. J., Mößle, T., & O'Brien, C. P. (2014). An international consensus for assessing internet gaming disorder using the new DSM-5 approach. *Addiction*, *109*(9), 1399–1406.

Ravaja, N., Salminen, M., Holopainen, J., Saari, T., Laarni, J., & Järvinen, A. (2004, October). Emotional response patterns and sense of presence during video games: Potential criterion variables for game design. In Proceedings of the third Nordic conference on Human-computer interaction (pp. 339–347). ACM.

Russoniello, C. V., O'Brien, K., & Parks, J. M. (2009). The effectiveness of casual video games in improving mood and decreasing stress. *Journal of Cyber Therapy and Rehabilitation*, *2*(1), 53–66.

Sanghavi, D. (2012). Are TV and video games making kids fat? *Slate.com*. http://www.slate.com/articles/health_and_science/medical_examiner/2012/04/are_video_games_making_kids_fat_screen_time_and_childhood_obesity_.html

Singh, M. (2014). Less sleep, more time online raise risk for teen depression. *NPR.org*. http://www.npr.org/blogs/health/2014/02/06/272441146/less-sleep-more-time-online-amp-up-teen-depression-risk

Skoric, M. M., Teo, L. L. C., & Neo, R. L. (2009). Children and video games: addiction, engagement, and scholastic achievement. *Cyberpsychology & Behavior*, *12*(5), 567–572.

Stettler, N., Signer, T. M., & Suter, P. M. (2004). Electronic games and environmental factors associated with childhood obesity in Switzerland. *Obesity Research, 12*(6), 896–903.

Thompson, D., Baranowski, T., Buday, R., Baranowski, J., Thompson, V., Jago, R., & Griffith, M. J. (2008). Serious video games for health: how behavioral science guided the design of a game on diabetes and obesity. *Simulation & Gaming, 41*(4) 587–606.

Valadez, J. J., & Ferguson, C. J. (2012). Just a game after all: Violent video game exposure and time spent playing effects on hostile feelings, depression, and visuospatial cognition. *Computers in Human Behavior, 28*(2), 608–616.

Vandewater, E. A., Shim, M. S., & Caplovitz, A. G. (2004). Linking obesity and activity level with children's television and video game use. *Journal of Adolescence, 27*(1), 71–85.

Weinstein, A. M. (2010). Computer and video game addiction—a comparison between game users and non-game users. *The American Journal of Drug and Alcohol Abuse, 36*(5), 268–276.

Wenzel, H. G., Bakken, I. J., Johansson, A., Götestam, K. G., & Øren, A. (2009). Excessive computer game playing among Norwegian adults: Self-reported consequences of playing and association with mental health problems. *Psychological Reports, 105*(3), 1237–1247

Williams, D., Yee, N., & Caplan, S. E. (2008). Who plays, how much, and why? Debunking the stereotypical gamer profile. *Journal of Computer Mediated Communication, 13*(4), 993–1018.

Wood, R. T. (2008). Problems with the concept of video game "addiction": Some case study examples. *International Journal of Mental Health and Addiction, 6*(2), 169–178.

Chapter Twelve

Conclusion

Predictions and Future Trends

Thus far, this book has explored extant literature on different issues related to video games. From here, the book will make some predictions for trends related to these issues in video games.

Trend 1: Video Games Play a Major Role in Contemporary Society. This Role Will Expand in the Coming Years.

This is not likely a bold proposal. With the rise of mobile gaming, more and more people will have access to video games and accessibility can breed familiarity. The simple idea that the reach of video games will expand helps explain this prediction.

Beyond this, video games have proven to be financially lucrative, if not risky. This will make the game design space attractive to investors and entre-preneurs alike. Simultaneously, since video games entered the mainstream in the 1970s, more and more people have grown up with them. These two things in conjunction suggest that the role of video games will expand in the future as digital natives become more prevalent (Palfrey & Gasser, 2013; Prensky, 2001). Consequently, more people will be using video games for entertainment, education, and therapy, as well as many other applications. Indeed, the role of video games will become more prominent.

Trend 2: Feedback Will Become More Widespread as Will Interactivity. However, Both Concepts Will Continue to Have Conflicting or Inconsistent Definitions.

As noted in the introductory chapters of this book, interactivity is a buzz-word. The term seems to catch the attention of the masses. This alongside persistent technological advancements, the use of the term "interactivity" increases. Comparably, feedback, as demonstrated, is something that has an incredibly powerful influence on human behavior. This notion is influencing consumer product design trends (Goetz, 2011) and this trend should contin-ue. Recently, advertisements have run for the Nest thermostat. It is a learning thermostat that acclimates to the habits and preferences of the owners. In this instance, the thermostat creates a feedback loop because the desired tempera-ture is the goal and the owner provides input values. Nest is not unique, there are a handful of other consumer products that rely on and push the applica-tion of feedback as a basic design principle. Here are a few products as detailed by Goetz (2011):

- Zeo offers a headband that measures the user's brainwaves during sleep. The device provides feedback on the duration and quality of sleep. From there, the user can go on the product's website to get tips on how to improve his or her sleep.
- Belkin offers a device that connects an appliance to a wall outlet. This device measures the power consumption of that appliance. The power consumption is then converted into meaningful information for the user: how much it costs to run this appliance and how much carbon is emitted. The idea is that providing this feedback in a meaningful way will alter energy consumption behaviors.
- GreenGoose uses a feedback system in the form of points to encourage users to complete daily tasks on a regular basis. These tasks are typically minor chores or minor self-improvement activities.

More and more devices will, and should, look to video games for examples of effective feedback implementation. Effective feedback explains much of the appeal of video games and feedback can make many daily routines more fun, easier, and safer, but this implementation has yet to be optimized.

Despite the widespread use of the terms feedback and interactivity, defi-nitions of these terms will not become any clearer in the near future. In terms of interactivity, many of the conceptualizations appear to be at odds with one another. The user control conceptualization is parsimonious but can become easily conflated with other concepts tied to new media (Jensen, 1998; Sun-dar, Kalyanaraman, & Brown, 2003). Bucy's perspective that interactivity is perceptual is probably the most useful until a more thorough understanding of what constitutes interactivity is developed—this book takes the position that perceived interactivity is a different concept than interactivity and should be treated as such. As understanding and technology advances scholars should maintain close watch on how to define interactivity.

As for feedback, the term is widely used so a clear definition has been elusive. Indeed, there are competing typologies of feedback. Most commonly, feedback is qualified as positive or negative but the meaning of those terms is inconsistent. On one hand, positive and negative feedback have been defined in terms of performance evaluation and the corresponding emotional valence such that positive feedback (performing well) elicits positive emotions and negative feedback (performing poorly) elicits negative emotions (Connellan & Zemke, 1993; Hattie & Timperley, 2007; Reinecke et al., 2012). Under this paradigm, positive feedback is, "you did very well, keep up the good work" and negative feedback is, "you did poorly, you should try harder next time." On the other hand, positive and negative feedback can also refer to the direction the feedback funnels the discrepancy between the input value and the goal value (Ramaprasad, 1983; Carver & Scheier, 2001). Positive feedback drives the input values away from a specific value. Negative feedback reduces the discrepancy between the input values and a specific value. In other words, positive feedback is designed to make the discrepancy between an input and the reference value larger or "more positive" while negative feedback is designed to make the value of the discrepancy a smaller number, thus chipping away at a larger original output value.

This is but one example, however; other typologies are similarly problematic (see Hattie & Timperley, 2007; Haug et al., 2010; Hawkins, Kreuter, Resnicow, Fishbein, & Dijkstra, 2008; Kluger & DeNisi, 1996). Based on all of the conflicts, a more clear definition has been pushed aside. Ideally, this book provides a degree of clarity on what feedback is and what feedback *is not* despite these inconsistent typologies.

Trend 3: Self-Presentation in Virtual Environments Will Play a Much Larger Role in Society

Some of the most popular websites on the Internet, sites like *Facebook*, *Twitter*, and *Instagram*, are ones that emphasize self-presentation. On each of these sites, the user is encouraged to build and maintain an online persona. In other words, they are asked to engage in a form of self-presentation.

Concurrently, the digital landscape allows for certain industries to move online that could not do so before. For example, many businesses have online stores and universities across the country have started to push online course offerings because online classes allow for flexible times, lower costs, unlimited seating, and less demand on classroom space. Thus, the only interactions customers/students might have with one another and with the retailer/instructor, are accomplished through personas created for online interactions. As systems become more sophisticated, people will cultivate these personas even further than they do currently. These personas will become increasingly varied and complex based on the context of the self-presentation. In class, for example, students may try to seem like serious academics. Self-presentation in online classes will make portraying this version of the self that much easier for savvy students. Meanwhile, in other scenarios, the student can socialize in virtual environments and cultivate a gregarious self-presentation. In that fashion, more and more face-to-face interactions will be replaced by online interactions but those interactions will begin to more closely resemble face-to-face interactions even though they are malleable in profound ways. Accordingly, as virtual reality becomes more ubiquitous, self-presentation will become an even more nuanced area of study and interaction.

Trend 4: The Stigma that Surrounds Video Game Players Will Disappear

The stigma surrounding video games will dissipate over time without the use of awareness programs or activist groups. Again, video games are becoming more widespread. More and more people are playing video games. Thus, more people are becoming video game players. Once a group gains more power, it is more difficult for them to be stigmatized. Correspondingly, the line between casual and hardcore video games will become increasingly blurred and the notion will be progressively subjective. Given the complexity of modern games, it stands to reason that future video games will be able to fill multiple roles that appeal to players on casual and hardcore levels such that people can play the same game with parameters that fit their preferences. There is already a degree of this. In the opening of *Child of Light* and *The Witcher III*, the player selects whether he or she wants to experience the game casually or as a challenge. This dichotomy is not explicit in other games though it is present. For example, many people may play *Call of Duty* casually but many others may play it professionally. In that way, the game has robust enough content that it allows the player to determine whether their experience will be casual or hardcore. Or, like Bucy's definition of interactivity, whether or not a game is hardcore or casual may be perceptual.

Furthermore, the video game industry is beginning to seep into other popular industries. Many professional athletes and celebrities regularly tweet about their love of video games. Just before Super Bowl XLIX, Rob Gronkowski of the New England Patriots and Marshawn Lynch of the Seattle Seahawks were on the late night talk show *Conan* playing a video game, *Mortal Kombat X*. This segment demonstrated that high profile celebrities, even athletes at the height of competition, are consuming these games. Beyond that, these celebrities are relatively wealthy and successful, two things not typically associated with video game players.

These are signs that video games are entering the mainstream even more so than they already have. Moreover, media portrayals of the video game player stereotype will be challenged more frequently; the Gronkowski and Lynch anecdote above is a prime example of this. Consequently, the reinforcement and accessibility of negative gamer stereotypes will decrease.

On the content producing side, building video games can make one wealthy and influential in certain circles. Gabe Newell, Cliff Bleszinski, and Hideo Kojima are all video game designers who are treated like celebrities by some. Players argue about which designer is the best and devote time and money to consume these designers' products. As these power dynamics shift and designers are viewed akin to celebrities, the stigmatization of video game players will shift as well.

Trend 5: The Application of Educational Video Games Will Expand Dramatically

There will be more games for education and more implementation of games in education in the coming years. Technology in classrooms is often heralded as the next great advancement in education (Bates, 2000; Kent & McNergney, 1999). Despite this, technology is absent from many lesson plans (Torrente, Moreno-Ger, Martínez-Ortiz, & Fernandez-Manjon, 2009). This is due, in large part, to perceived barriers in implementing technology and a lack of clear methods for implementation (Rogers, 2012; Fabry & Higgs, 1997). Accordingly, a question arises: How do we implement technology in the classroom?

This issue will resolve itself before long. Currently, many instructors are digital immigrants (Prensky, 2001) not digital natives (Palfrey & Gasser, 2013); meaning that many instructors are not comfortable, confident with, or accustomed to using games in the classroom. This is a problem albeit a smaller one for students because they tend to be digital natives. As time progresses, digital natives will assume instructor roles and the new students will be even more adept with technology. Consequently, the implementation of video games in the classroom will encounter fewer impediments.

Concurrently, designing video games for education will become more lucrative and, in turn, more educational games will be developed. In doing so, players will be immersed in and engaged with their lessons. The best way to work toward this end is to develop course-specific guidelines for using games (Rogers, 2012). It is not enough to put a game into a classroom and expect results but rather the rules, feedback, and self-presentation should be implemented to teach specific course lessons.

Trend 6: Games Will Be Used for Therapeutic Purposes More Commonly

Like education, there is already a lot of evidence that suggests video games are valuable health intervention tools. For example, games are thought to offer players the promise for better, happier, and more fulfilling lives (McGonigal, 2011) and could therefore be used to treat unhealthy mood states. Games can also be used to help treat and manage diabetes, obesity, and asthma (Kahol, 2011; Thompson et al., 2008; Vilozni et al., 2005). Video games can be used to encourage healthy eating and cardiovascular health (O'Donovan & Hussey, 2012; Pollak et al., 2010). For reasons similar to those outlined above (profitability, ubiquity of games, and increasing familiarity with games), uses for video games will increase in entertaining and healthy domains.

Trend 7: Video Game Addiction Will Become Widely Recognized and Diagnosed

Video game addiction is a widely used term but not officially recognized. In fact, the American Psychological Association still does not officially recognize it but "internet gaming disorder" is recognized (Petry et al., 2014). Moreover, the notion of video game addiction comes with several caveats. For example, the causality between video games and addiction is noted to be suspect and the disorder may actually be contingent upon factors outside of the games themselves. Since video games do not actually introduce a foreign chemical into the body, there has been resistance to classifying video games as an addiction.

Comparably, there is a debate concerning gambling addiction such that it might be considered an impulse control disorder *or* it might actually alter brain activity in ways that are closer to chemical dependency (Blanco, Moreyra, Nunes, Saiz-Ruiz, & Ibanez, 2001). As mentioned previously, receiving feedback is pleasurable. In other words, receiving feedback can prompt certain chemical releases in the brain. It seems plausible that a dependency on these dopamine releases as well as a developed tolerance for these dopamine releases could encourage a player to seek more intense releases in the future. Therefore, there are some arguments in favor of classifying video game addiction more formally.

The evidence on this topic will likely expand in the coming years and provide a more concrete conclusion. Furthermore, even though there are those who are skeptical that video game addiction exists, it has entered the American lexicon and, for that reason alone, will become more widespread.

Trend 8: Games Will Be Used to Stimulate Complex Moral Questions

As discussed previously, video games allow players to experience complex moral scenarios in which they must make a decision. Borrowing from the computers as social actors paradigm, this is an effective way to mirror experiences in the physical world (Le, Funk, & Hu, 2013; Reeves & Nass, 1996).

This has applications for education such that students in ethics courses could be placed in morally ambiguous scenarios. This could evaluate their knowledge of an industry's standards and practices. For example, a journalism student could be placed in a situation built to test his or her knowledge of how to conduct him or herself while reporting a story. Medical doctors or those in medical training positions can simulate difficult decisions and difficult conversations with patients or patients' families through games. The military can use games in a similar capacity and put soldiers into combat scenarios or non-combat personnel interactions. These simulations should allow various professionals to feel more confident and experienced when faced with difficult decisions in the workplace.

Trend 9: Concerns Related to Video Games and Violence Will Incorporate Concerns about Mental Illness

After the shooting at Sandy Hook was linked to video game play, President Obama delivered a speech indicating an initiative to further fund research on video game violence in order to reduce gun violence. One year later a video game website referred to Obama's speech as grandstanding (Rose, 2014) because we have had no sea change developments related to the relationship between video games and violence.

In moments of tragedy, the public often looks for answers even when those answers are elusive. While the evidence suggests that video games can impact aggression, it is also likely that video games have become a convenient explanation for violent tragedy even when that explanation may be oversimplified. Despite some of the terrific research done on the topic, there is not a complete picture of how violent video games impact those with mental illness. Exploring video games and mental illness is a fruitful area of inquiry in terms of preventing video game-related acts of violence. As understanding of video games advances, mental illness should be a larger part of the conversation.

POLICY AND PREDICTIONS

This portion of the book will look ahead at policy and discuss potential policy changes that may be impending and will examine policy from two discrete perspectives: legal policy and content producer policy.

Prediction 1: The Rules Related to Video Games and Virtual Environments Will Become Much Stricter

Throughout this book, notably in the rules section, certain rule infractions, illegal and legal, have been detailed. Infractions of rules will likely become more heavily regulated from a legal standpoint and from a game producer standpoint. The line between virtual crime and real crime has become more and more blurred. A degree of this is already seen in terms of virtual goods translating into actual dollar values. Many video game publishers opt for digital distribution of products as it reduces production and shipping costs while allowing the publisher to control resale of the physical copy of a game. That is, when used video game retailers like GameStop sell a used copy of a game, the game designers do not attain any of the money from the used sale. As a result, digital distribution allows companies to make more money by cutting out sale of physical copies of used games. As such, the games industry is putting an emphasis on virtual goods such that players are buying licenses to play the game rather than a copy of the game itself.

Simultaneously, game publishers have begun to release supplemental content that is an additional fee. For example, in game of the year winner *Dragon Age: Inquisition* players can pay an additional $10 on top of the video game's base price in order to access new weapons and armor. When these features are not locked behind paywalls, they are available after certain in-game tasks are accomplished. Often these unlocks take many hours of play. For example, in the video game *Evolve* a user must play the game for many hours to unlock all of the content. While it is much more difficult to put a dollar amount on the time a player spends unlocking content than on a product that has a physical world analogue, there is an intangible value of these items based on how much time and effort goes into gaining them. As this value becomes transmutable and more widely understood, more strict guidelines related to virtual goods will be enforced.

Additionally, harassment/cyberbullying laws will increase their reach into video games. As discussed, many video games feature harassment in multiplayer settings. Given the broad increase in concerns related to bullying behaviors, these behaviors will likely be under much more scrutiny in the coming years, especially as more people become aware of the vitriol used in many of these games. Much of this regulation will take the shape of a more widely understood etiquette in video games, as well as policies from individual server managers, as opposed to legal means of preventing the behavior.

Prediction 2: The Regulation of Violent Video Game Content is Not Likely in the United States

The recent decision of the Supreme Court of the United States to *not* regulate violent video games was a long-awaited, highly impactful decision. This decision put much of the debate to rest after decades of speculation and litigation. As a result, it is unlikely that this landmark decision will be altered in the near future.

However, caveats to this regulation will be found. This is especially applicable with the emergence of new technologies that will allow regulations to eschew the definition of video games. For example, when a video game uses virtual reality technology and haptic devices, there may be attempted regulations based on the technology as opposed to video game or content, as content is given a large degree of protection in the United States.

Prediction 3: Video Games Will Be a Major Part of the Net Neutrality Debate

Recently, the Federal Communications Commission voted on net neutrality rules. Essentially, these rules prevent Internet service providers from blocking certain content to customers. Also, it requires that all customers receive the same Internet speed. These rules have been controversial and are likely going to be the subject of much debate in the coming months or even years. To summarize the debate, some see the net neutrality rules as ensuring consumer protection while others view these rules as unnecessary regulation that could potentially stifle entrepreneurship.

Regardless of the politics involved, video games will be and should be a major part of this discussion. The broadband usage of video games is high. Many video games have downloads or online modes that require high Internet speeds. In this fashion, video game players might be using and requiring much faster Internet speeds than other non-gaming Internet users. As a result, this should be a consideration for both sides of the debate. On one hand, low Internet speeds should not prevent some from experiencing video games, especially educational and therapeutic games. On the other hand, online video game players will be using much more of the resource than others, yet paying the same fees.

Prediction 4: The Surveillance of Game Play Will Increase

In 2013, Edward Snowden leaked information regarding the National Security Agency's surveillance program. This program contained unprecedented and unimaginable levels of surveillance that extended to video game play. It is already known that players of *World of Warcraft* as well as other games were under government surveillance because the NSA believed that video games provided a platform for terrorists to communicate (Gross, 2013). Microsoft, the creator of the Xbox consoles, also provided the NSA with access to their users' messages and behaviors (Greenwald, MacAskill, Poitras, Ackerman, & Rushe, 2013).

Given the ability for video games to connect groups, train individuals, and embed players within certain epistemological frameworks (discussed earlier in this book), it stands to reason that video games could be tools for terrorists to recruit and train. This is and will likely continue to be used to justify surveillance of video game players. On top of that, video game content often pushes the boundaries of what is deemed socially and morally acceptable. Some of these games, like *JFK: Reloaded*, *Rapelay*, and *Super Columbine Massacre RPG!!!* have been discussed in previous chapters. It seems reasonable that in the same way the NSA is likely to track people who search certain terms online, the NSA will also track people who play certain games, especially when those games have an ideological message that might be related to terrorism or acts of violence.

The degree of the surveillance will be determined by the new technology used by games. Both the Sony Playstation and the Microsoft Xbox can be used with cameras that peer into the homes of players. There is reason to believe that the NSA can peek into players' living rooms using these cameras. When—rather than if—games begin to track physiological measures and brain activity, the NSA will be able to access that information as well. These advancements will provide exciting opportunities for video game experiences but players should be aware that this information is not likely to be private.

Prediction 5: Video Games Will Be Increasingly Intertwined with Obesity Policy

Obesity has reached epidemic level in the United States. Even First Lady Michelle Obama made the issue of childhood obesity a priority with her Let's Move! campaign. As discussed earlier, video games have been linked to issues of obesity although there has not been much strong causal evidence linking video game play and obesity. Despite this, it should not be surprising to find video games and obesity more inextricably linked, especially in terms of policy. Policy related to curbing obesity will more frequently refer to and give advice on video game play. These policies will impact the video game market and alter the way games are made.

Prediction 6: Video Game Content Will Become More Violent, More Sexual, and More Realistic

Video games already include a large degree of violent and sexual content. However, content producers will include *more* violent and sexual content as time goes on, following trends of other industries (Walsh & Gentile, 2001). Some pornographic video games already exist and there will be more in the future. In fact, there will be more sexual content than violent content as video game technology advances in terms of haptics and immersion. The desire to experience immersive, multisensory sexual content will be greater than the desire to experience immersive, multisensory violent content. Violent content may change in order to make it more palatable in these immersive contexts. That is, players will be more interested in deeply feeling virtual sexual experiences than violent experiences.

On this point, the video game industry, in its broad pursuit of realism, will shift from photorealism *to* realism in the form of more immersive experiences. Emphasis will continue on graphical and audio fidelity but these will plateau as photorealism has more or less been achieved. In turn, more technology will be implemented that creates more immersive experiences through virtual reality and haptics.

Prediction 7: Video Games Will Become More and More Customized and Video Games Will Teach Other Industries How to Customize Effectively

The benefits of customized content are well documented in many domains such as health interventions (Lustria, Cortese, Noar, & Glueckauf, 2009; Noar, Crosby, Benac, Snow, & Troutman, 2011; Rimer & Kreuter, 2006) and new media platforms/products (Ansari & Mela, 2003; Kalyanaraman & Sundar, 2006; Kamali & Loker, 2002). Customization is defined as individualized content, as opposed to generic content (Kalyanaraman & Sundar, 2006; Wheeler, DeMarree, & Petty, 2008; Wheeler, Petty, & Bizer, 2005), that caters to "some aspect of the self" (Briñol & Petty, 2006, p. 583). Customization, personalization, matching, and tailoring are closely related but have nuanced definitions (Hawkins, Kreuter, Resnicow, Fishbein, & Dijkstra, 2008; Latimer, Katulak, Mowad, & Salovey, 2005; Lustria et al., 2009; Noar, Benac, & Harris, 2007; Park, McDaniel, & Jung, 2009; Rimer & Kreuter, 2006; Sundar & Marathe, 2010).

While these differences have been explored, much less is known about differences between types of customization. Largely, customization has been treated as a monolithic concept but video games provide evidence that there are a variety of types of customization. Avatar customization typically takes place in the early stages of video game play, but the method of avatar creation is not uniform across all games. Some games force players to use a specific avatar with a fixed appearance or abilities while others offer robust avatar customization allowing players to change the appearance and abilities of their avatars to specifically fit the player's preference. Appearance is often manipulated via facial structures, hairstyle, skin tone, eye color, clothing, etc. Abilities are typically customized by selecting specific skills like speed, strength, enabling item use, or attributing skill points, as a player prefers. This is common in best-selling games like *Call of Duty* and *World of Warcraft*.

One of the studies that best examines multiple types of customization did so by asking participants to describe the avatar they wanted to use based on the big five personality factors: openness, conscientiousness, extraversion, agreeableness, and neuroticism (Trepte & Reinecke, 2010). While this method of avatar creation is not directly applicable to existing video games, this study highlights the importance of avatar customization on multiple dimensions. Similarly, the clearest evidence provided on the differences between ability and appearance customization can be found in a survey (Turkay & Adinolf, 2010). According to this survey, customizing avatar appearance was related to enjoyment of a game while ability customization was not.

In order to more fully parse these differences three studies tested different types of customization (Rogers, 2015). In the first study participants were told that they were designing an avatar for playing a new, open world, action/role-playing game. Importantly, this game was fictional and participants never played this game but designed an avatar under the impression that they would play this game.

Analysis revealed no main effects of appearance customization and ability customization on attitude toward the game. However, further analysis revealed that appearance customization impacted feelings of authorship and identification with the character while ability customization only impacted feelings of authorship. Notably, those using appearance customization felt a greater sense of authorship than those customizing ability. While there were no direct effects of customization on attitude toward the game, the indirect effects of appearance customization on attitude were significant via identification such that when users were able to customize their avatar's appearance they identified with the avatar and that identification led to more positive attitudes toward the game.

In the second study actual game play was used as the lack of game play in the first study may have blunted the impact of ability customization. The game was a side scrolling platformer where players used the arrow keys on the computer keyboard to control a pig's movement. The object of the game was to jump over pitfalls and enemies while also bouncing a ball on the pig's head/back.

There were no effects of appearance customization and ability customization on attitude toward the game by themselves but there were when taken in conjunction such that people liked the game more when they could customize both appearance and ability. Meanwhile, appearance customization positively predicted feelings of authorship and identification. Ability customization only had an impact on authorship. Again, there were no direct effects of either independent variable on attitude. However, the indirect effects via identification for appearance customization on attitude were significant when users also had the ability to customize abilities.

As suspected, the impact of ability customization was more pronounced when the player got to use the skills but its impact was still tenuous. Consequently, a third and final study on this topic was performed. In this study participants played a soccer simulator in which players controlled a player in a soccer game from a top down view. The player was controlled with the mouse and keyboard. The object of the game was to win the soccer match.

Analysis for this study showed that appearance customization had a positive impact on attitude toward the game but ability customization had no impact. In this instance appearance customization positively impacted feelings of authorship and identification. Ability customization did not predict either of these. Here the feelings of authorship did not lead to positive attitudes toward the game but feelings of identification did.

In sum, these three studies show that different types of customization do impact users discretely with appearance customization seeming to have benefits over ability customization. The effects of ability customization only emerged in specific gameplay scenarios and when appearance customization was enabled as well.

These findings in conjunction with existing avatar research detailed previously (Klimmt, Hefner, & Vorderer, 2009; Peña, Hancock, & Merola, 2009; Yee & Bailenson, 2007; Yee, Bailenson, & Ducheneaut, 2009) indicate that the user is more likely to merge psychologically with a character when the character is customizable and this merger translates into value for the consumer.

This series of studies highlights that how a character appears is much more important than what a character can do. In other words, it is easier for a user to assume the role of a media character and psychologically merge with that character when they can customize the avatar's appearance as opposed to its abilities. It seems that avatar customization is only as effective as the psychological merger it engenders and appearance customization is more effective in doing so than ability customization. These studies help to further understanding of the nuances of customization in terms of video games, avatars, and consumer behavior. Also, these studies demonstrate the mechanisms of customization in video games. In the current media landscape, a large degree of content can be tailored to the individual and thereby increase the appeal/value of that content, and video games offer insight into best practices for implementing customization in other domains.

Prediction 8: The Pattern of Digital Distribution Will Grow

Online purchases and e-commerce have become major markets. Digital distribution is on the rise. One major area of digital distribution is micropayments. Micropayments are typically understood as minor online purchases, around $12 (Paypal, 2014) or minor entertainment purchases such as downloadable music, games, and movies (Gedda, 2010). In video games, these sorts of micropayments are often referred to as microtransactions. Within the world of online gaming, microtransactions can take many forms, like buying virtual pets in *World of Warcraft* (Funk, 2009a), extra armor for your avatar (Ransom-Wiley, 2006), additional game play opportunities (Brudvig, 2009) and even subscription fees to pay for access to play games online (Funk, 2009b). This model is used because game studios can make more money off of a game. For example, before digital distribution, a game studio could make money off of a game only when the game was initially purchased. That is, the average revenue per user can be increased. Now, with digital distribution and microtransactions, players can spend more money on additional content that does not require a studio to produce a new full retail game. A similar pattern emerges with the free to play video games model. Under this model, content producers provide a game for free but there are many items in the game that a player must pay to acquire. That, or the game is monetized by including advertisements which fund the studio. Free to play video games also serve to combat piracy because providing a game for free lowers the likelihood that someone will pirate the game. As a result, video games can ultimately make more money using these business models than if the game is only sold as a physical copy at the original point of purchase.

Given this growing trend and the increasing ubiquity of microtransactions, it is as important as ever to cultivate an understanding of digital distribution systems. Based on this, a handful of exploratory studies on player perceptions of how microtransactions function within video games were performed (Rogers, 2015). Players were asked to rate how they felt about the dollar value of three different video games. In all three games, players indicated that they were willing to spend more money for game add-ons offered than they were willing to spend on the base game.

One item included examined how the ability to customize an avatar's appearance and ability should be valued. Interestingly, in each case, ability customization was considered more valuable than appearance customization. This demonstrates the inverse of the pattern detailed above. In other words, people *think* that ability customization is valuable when in fact, they have more positive attitudes toward appearance customization.

In light of this seeming paradox, the same study described in prediction 7 was run again but it examined the likelihood of making a microtransaction in place of attitude toward the game. When likelihood of making a microtransaction was entered as the outcome variable a similar pattern emerged as did previously. Again, appearance customization was driving most of the desire to make a microtransaction. Appearance customization led to more identification with the avatar, which led to a higher likelihood of making a microtransaction. These findings may mean that people *think* they want to customize ability features but in reality they prefer appearance customizing features in video games.

Based on this evidence, digital distribution, microtransactions, and the free to play model are all savvy business practices. Furthermore, the type of content offered is important as people demonstrate a preference for certain content in these contexts over others. The video game industry will likely adopt these tactics further in the coming years.

Prediction 9: Asynchronous Multiplayer Will Become More Prevalent

The video game industry has shown that it is innovative in that it finds ways to make its products appealing to many different kinds of players. One way video games can broaden their appeal is through more use of asynchronous multiplayer. Asynchronous multiplayer allows people to play a game without being tied to a specific location for a specific period of time. For example, if one wanted to play *Halo* with friends, he or she would have to try to coordinate a time with friends to play, sit on his or her couch when the friends are available, and play for the time they had set aside. Meanwhile, if one wanted to play *Words with Friends*, he or she can take a turn when he or she has the opportunity. For those not familiar with those games, perhaps the most illustrative example is playing chess by mail. This expands the reach of video games and also extends their flexibility, allowing players to play more conveniently and accessibly. In doing so, video games can appeal to and reach more players.

In Conclusion

To conclude the book, a brief summary is provided. Many of the most relevant issues in video games have been reviewed. Some are positive and some are negative but all deserve more attention. This book posits that through special attention to feedback, rules, and self-presentation, an understanding of how video games impact people can be cultivated while maximizing the positive outcomes in video games and minimizing the negative outcomes.

Likewise, the video game industry and video game policy makers should look to these concepts for clarity on social issues.

In closing, this book argues that video games are impacting people in all kinds of ways but these notions require more exploration, especially as video games and their technology advance.

REFERENCES

Ansari, A., & Mela, C. F. (2003). E-customization. *Journal of Marketing Research, 40*(2), 131–145.

Bates, A. W. (2000). *Managing technological change: Strategies for college and university leaders*. San Francisco: Jossey-Bass.

Blanco, C., Moreyra, P., Nunes, E. V., Saiz-Ruiz, J., & Ibanez, A. (2001). Pathological gambling: addiction or compulsion?. *Seminars in Clinical Neuropsychiatry*, *6*(3), 167–176.

Briñol, P., & Petty, R. E. (2006). Fundamental processes leading to attitude change: Implications for cancer prevention communications. *Journal of Communication, 56*, S81–S104.

Brudvig, E. (2009). Fallout 3: Mothership Zeta review. *IGN*. http://xboxlive.ign.com/articles/101/1010543p1.html

Bucy, E. (2004). Interactivity in society: Locating an elusive concept. *Information Society*, *20*(5), 373–383.

Carver, C., & Scheier, M. (2001). *On the self-regulation of behavior*. Cambridge: Cambridge University Press.

Connellan, T., & Zemke, R. (1993). *Sustaining knock your socks off service*. New York: AMACOM Books.

Fabry, D. L., & Higgs, J. R. (1997). Barriers to the effective use of technology in education: Current status. *Journal of Educational Computing Research, 17*(4), 385–395.

Funk, J. (2009b). A view from the road: How I learned to stop worrying and love the microtransaction. *The Escapist Magazine*. http://www.escapistmagazine.com/articles/view/columns/view-from-the-road/6330-A-View-from-the-Road-How-I-Learned-to-Stop-Worrying-and-Love-the-Microtransaction.2

Funk, J. (2009a). *World of Warcraft* gets microtransaction pets, players freak out. *The Escapist Magazine*. http://www.escapistmagazine.com/news/view/95927-World-of-Warcraft-Gets-Microtransaction-Pets-Players-Freak-Out

Gedda, R. (2010). Visa's payclick takes on PayPal for micropayments. *Techworld*.com. http://www.techworld.com.au/article/351015/visa_payclick_takes_paypal_micropayments/

Goetz, T. (2011). Harnessing the power of feedback loops. *Wired*. http://www.wired.com/magazine/2011/06/ff_feedbackloop/

Greenwald, G., MacAskill, E., Poitras, L., Ackerman, S., & Rushe, D. (2013). Microsoft handed the NSA access to encrypted messages. *The Guardian.com*. http://www.theguardian.com/world/2013/jul/11/microsoft-nsa-collaboration-user-data

Gross, D. (2013). Leak: Government spies snooped in 'Warcraft,' other games. *CNN.com*. http://www.cnn.com/2013/12/09/tech/web/nsa-spying-video-games/index.html

Hattie, J., & Timperley, H. (2007). The power of feedback. *Review of Educational Research, 77*(1), 81–112.

Haug, S., Meyer, C., Ulbricht, S., Gross, B., Rumpf, H., & John, U. (2010). Need for cognition as a predictor and a moderator of outcome in a tailored letters smoking cessation intervention. *Health Psychology, 29*(4), 367–373.

Hawkins, R. P., Kreuter, M., Resnicow, K., Fishbein, M., & Dijkstra, A. (2008). Understanding tailoring in communicating about health. *Health Education Research, 23*(3), 454–466.

Jensen, J. F. (1998). Interactivity: Tracking a new concept in media and communication studies. *Nordicom Review, 19*, 185–204.

Kahol, K. (2011). Integrative gaming: A framework for sustainable game-based diabetes management. *Journal of Diabetes Science and Technology, 5*(2), 293–300.

Kalyanaraman, S., & Sundar, S. (2006). The psychological appeal of personalized content in web portals: Does customization affect attitudes and behavior?. *Journal of Communication*, *56*(1), 110–132.

Kamali, N., & Loker, S. (2002). Mass customization: On-line consumer involvement in product design. *Journal of Computer-Mediated Communication*, *7*(4).

Kent, T. W., & McNergney, R. F. (1999). *Will technology really change education? From blackboard to web*. Thousand Oaks, CA: Corwin Press.

Klimmt, C., Hefner, D., & Vorderer, P. (2009). The videogame experience as "true" identification: A theory of enjoyable alterations of players' self-perception. *Communication Theory*, *19*, 351–373.

Kluger, A. N., & DeNisi, A. (1996). The effects of feedback interventions on performance: A historical review, a meta-analysis and a preliminary feedback intervention theory. *Psychological Bulletin*, *119*, 254–284.

Latimer, A. E., Katulak, N. A., Mowad, L., & Salovey, P. (2005). Motivating cancer prevention and early detection behaviors using psychologically tailored messages. *Journal of Health Communication*, *10*, 137–155.

Le, D., Funk, M., & Hu, J. (2013). Blobulous: Computers As Social Actors. *In CHI 2013 Workshop on Experiencing Interactivity in Public Spaces* EIPS, Paris

Lustria, M. L., Cortese, J., Noar, S. M., & Glueckauf, R. L. (2009). Computer-tailored health interventions delivered over the web: Review and analysis of key components. *Patient Education & Counseling*, *74*(2), 156–173.

McGonigal, J. (2011). Reality is broken: Why games make us better and how they can change the world. New York: Penguin.

Noar, S. M., Benac, C. N., & Harris, M. S. (2007). Does tailoring matter? Meta-analytic review of tailored print health behavior change interventions. *Psychological Bulletin*, *133*(4), 673–693.

Noar, S., Crosby, R., Benac, C., Snow, G., & Troutman, A. (2011). Application of the attitude-social influence-efficacy model to condom use among African-American STD clinic patients: Implications for tailored health communication. *AIDS & Behavior*, *15*(5), 1045–1057.

O'Donovan, C., & Hussey, J. (2012). Active video games as a form of exercise and the effect of gaming experience: A preliminary study in healthy young adults. *Physiotherapy*, *98*(3), 205–210.

Palfrey, J., & Gasser, U. (2013). *Born digital: Understanding the first generation of digital natives*. New York: Basic Books.

Park, E., McDaniel, A., & Jung, M. S. (2009). Computerized tailoring of health information. *CIN: Computers, Informatics, Nursing*, *27*(1), 34–43.

Paypal (2014). Micropayments. *Paypal.com*. Retrieved from https://www.paypal.com/uk/webapps/mpp/micropayments

Peña, J., Hancock, J. T., & Merola, N. A. (2009). The priming effects of avatars in virtual settings. *Communication Research*, *36*(6), 838–856.

Petry, N. M., Rehbein, F., Gentile, D. A., Lemmens, J. S., Rumpf, H. J., Mößle, T., & O'Brien, C. P. (2014). An international consensus for assessing internet gaming disorder using the new DSM-5 approach. *Addiction*, *109*(9), 1399–1406.

Pollak, J., Gay, G., Byrne, S., Wagner, E., Retelny, D., & Humphreys, L. (2010). It's time to eat! Using mobile games to promote healthy eating. *Pervasive Computing, IEEE*, *9*(3), 21–27.

Prensky, M. (2001). Digital natives, digital immigrants part 1. *On the Horizon*, *9*(5), 1–6.

Ramaprasad, A. (1983). On the definition of feedback. *Behavioral Science*, *28*(1).

Ransom-Wiley, J. (2006). Download Oblivion's horse armor, for a price. *Joystiq*. http://www.joystiq.com/2006/04/03/download-oblivions-horse-armor-for-a-price/

Reeves, B. & Nass, C., (1996). *The media equation: How people treat computers, televisions, and new media as real people and places*. Cambridge: Cambridge University Press.

Reinecke, L., Tamborini, R., Grizzard, M., Lewis, R., Eden, A., & Bowman, N. (2012). Characterizing mood management as need satisfaction: The effects of intrinsic needs on selective exposure and mood repair. *Journal of Communication*, *62*(3), 437–453.

Rimer, B. K., & Kreuter, M. W. (2006). Advancing tailored health communication: A persuasion and message effects perspective. *Journal of Communication, 56,* S184–S201.

Rogers, R. (2015). Appearance and ability: The impact of different types of avatar customization. Unpublished manuscript, Department of Communication, Marist College, Poughkeepsie, New York.

Rogers, R. (2012). Broadcast journalism lessons in video games. *Academic Exchange Quarterly, 16*(2).

Rose, M. (2014). Video games and gun violence: A year after Sandy Hook. *Gamasutra.com.* http://www.gamasutra.com/view/feature/210322/video_games_and_gun_violence_a_.php

Sundar, S., Kalyanaraman, S., & Brown, J. (2003). Explicating web site interactively: Impression formation effects in political campaign sites. *Communication Research, 30*(1), 30–59.

Sundar, S. S., & Marathe, S. S. (2010). Personalization versus customization: The importance of agency, privacy, and power usage. *Human Communication Research, 36*(3), 298–322.

Thompson, D., Baranowski, T., Buday, R., Baranowski, J., Thompson, V., Jago, R., & Griffith, M. J. (2008). Serious video games for health: How behavioral science guided the design of a game on diabetes and obesity. *Simulation & Gaming, 41*(4) 587–606.

Torrente, J., Moreno-Ger, P., Martínez-Ortiz, I., & Fernandez-Manjon, B. (2009). Integration and deployment of educational games in e-learning environments: The learning object model meets educational gaming. *Journal of Educational Technology & Society, 12*(4), 359–371.

Trepte, S., & Reinecke, L. (2010). Avatar creation and video game enjoyment: Effects of life-satisfaction, game competitiveness, and identification with the avatar. *Journal of Media Psychology: Theories, Methods, and Applications, 22*(4), 171–184.

Turkay, S., & Adinolf, S. (2010). Free to be me: A survey study on customization with World of Warcraft and City Of Heroes/Villains players. *Procedia Social and Behavioral Sciences, 2* (2010), 1840–1845.

Vilozni, D., Barak, A., Efrati, O., Augarten, A., Springer, C., Yahav, Y., & Bentur, L. (2005). The role of computer games in measuring spirometry in healthy and "asthmatic" preschool children. *Chest Journal, 128*(3), 1146–1155.

Walsh, D. A., & Gentile, D. A. (2001). A validity test of movie, television, and video-game ratings. *Pediatrics, 107*(6), 1302–1308.

Wheeler, S. C., DeMarree, K. G., & Petty, R. E. (2008). A match made in the laboratory: Persuasion and matches to primed traits and stereotypes. *Journal of Experimental Social Psychology, 44*(4), 1035–1047.

Wheeler, S. C., Petty, R. E., & Bizer, G. Y. (2005). Self-schema matching and attitude change: Situational and dispositional determinants of message elaboration. *Journal of Consumer Research, 31*(4), 787–797.

Yee, N., & Bailenson, J. (2007). The Proteus effect: The effect of transformed self-representation on behavior. *Human Communication Research, 33*(3), 271–290.

Yee, N., Bailenson, J. N., & Ducheneaut, N. (2009). The Proteus effect: Implications of transformed digital self-representation on online and offline behavior. *Communication Research, 36,* 285–312.

Index

About the Author

Ryan Rogers has earned a BA from the University of Notre Dame, a MA from the S.I. Newhouse School of Public Communications at Syracuse University and a PhD in Mass Communication from the University of North Carolina at Chapel Hill. He is currently an assistant professor at Marist College. His research interests center on the psychology of human-technology interaction, with particular attention to video game environments.